Praise for
HOW TO BE UNLUCKY

How To Be Unlucky is a much needed book, a book which will prove spiritually and intellectually valuable to teachers, students, and parents alike. This book stands to significantly change the way you think of education. As a professor, I'd love for all of my colleagues to be drinking deeply of the ideas Joshua Gibbs is tackling in *How to Be Unlucky*. Our rising generation obviously needs to be wrestling more regularly with both the theory and practice of virtue, but how can we get them to want to? Mere moralistic lecturing probably makes the outcome we seek less rather than more likely, so what is to be done? Well, here's some good news: Both wit and wise counsel—and an introductory guide to the ancients, and some self-deprecation about Gibbs's own failures, and even meaningful reflection on 1990s rock—all await you in these important pages."
—Senator Ben Sasse, author of *The Vanishing American Adult*

With poetic, honest, and compelling prose, *How to Be Unlucky* calls readers to reject the siren songs of material success and worldly pleasures, and to pursue instead the only things that matter: wisdom, virtue, and godliness. The world needs more books like this and more of the virtues Joshua Gibbs teaches and models in these pages.
—Karen Swallow Prior, author of *On Reading Well*

Reading Joshua Gibbs is thought-provoking, challenging, inspiring, and with-al, practical. This book made me want to go back to high school and sit in his class. Finally! A teacher who understands that teaching great books, big ideas, critical thinking, writing techniques, and all that are simply means to the end of practicing virtue and laying up treasure in heaven. Had I read this book when I started teaching, I would have been a much better (and more honest and brave) teacher.
—David Hicks, author of *Norms and Nobility*

Something They
Will Not Forget

SOMETHING THEY WILL NOT FORGET

A Handbook for Classical Teachers

Joshua Gibbs

CiRCE
Concord, NC

Published in the USA
by the CiRCE Institute
© 2019 Joshua Gibbs

ISBN: 978-0-9991466-7-5

For information:
CiRCE Institute
81 McCachern Blvd.
Concord, NC 28025
www.circeinstitute.org

Cover design by Graeme Pitman.

Printed in the United States of America.

For Robyn Burlew and Keith Nix.

Thanks for the leeway.

Contents

W hat's a nice, non-liturgical Baptist, public school educated girl like me—who was never required to memorize anything longer than her phone number—doing here, writing a foreword for a book like this? What do I know about catechism, memorization, or classical Christian education?

Well, with the benefit of over half a century's worth of hindsight, I know a little bit about what I missed by not memorizing more. And with nearly three decades of teaching experience behind me, I know what many of my own students are lacking, too. Besides, just because I wasn't formally catechized or officially required to memorize much doesn't mean that such things didn't occur anyway. In fact, quite the opposite is true.

From sheer voluntary, frequent repetition, I remember—with joy—almost every line from the first book I learned to read: *Hand, Hand, Fingers, Thumb* by Al Perkins.

As a result of the many Sundays of my early years spent in rural Baptist churches, I remember the first, second, and last stanzas of countless hymns—the good ("Come, Ye Sinners, Poor and Needy"), the bad ("I Come to the Garden Alone"), and the ugly ("Are You Washed in the Blood?"). And I have hid in my heart many Bible verses (mostly in the English of King James), despite the fact that I don't remember being told to memorize them nor how or when I did so.

To this day, I remember many of the songs my entire fifth grade sang in the elaborate musical we performed in celebration of America's bicentennial—as well as the single dependent clause that constituted my one speaking part.

As an adolescent, I memorized Robert Frost's "Nothing Gold Can Stay" because I loved so much the book in which I first encountered it, S.E. Hinton's, *The Outsiders*.

So as it turns out, most—if not all—of my memorization during my schooling years was accidental.

I've always secretly wished I had memorized much more: more Bible verses, more poetry, more Shakespearean soliloquies (or even just one).

This is why, when I got my first full-time faculty appointment as an English professor nearly twenty years ago, when most of my classes were general education literature survey courses, I required my students to memorize a passage of their choosing from among the works we read. The students didn't have to memorize a great deal—two stanzas of a long poem or a paragraph from a prose work would do. They could recite the passage at the start of class on any day of their choosing. And when they were done, I asked them to explain why they chose that particular work or passage.

Years later, some students tell me that this memorization and recitation (especially the recitation) is the part of the class that has stayed with them the most. Some still have the passage memorized even after ten or more years. Some tell me they can no longer recite the passage—but they do remember which work they chose and why. One student reports that she used some of the same memorization techniques that she used for that assignment when her job required her to deliver briefings to high-level government officials. Other students who went on to become teachers themselves say that they now require this assignment of their own students.

As my former students attest from this simple act of memorization—and as Joshua Gibbs shows in greater expanse and depth in this book—the practices of catechesis, recitation, and memorization help turn the *information* offered by a teacher or textbook into *formation* of the student. Other pedagogical methods such as discussion, reflection, and writing, which also assist in such formation, work best when the mind has been filled and formed by good material which it can draw upon. Because our brains naturally memorize with sufficient repetition, we merely need to replace accident with intention in order to facilitate the memorization of good content and more of it.

Something They Will Not Forget helpfully provides excellent models and templates for classroom catechism. However, as the book so enticingly and convincingly shows, a catechetical education is about much more than memory storage. The practices of repetition, rumination, and reflection—punctuated by pauses and silence—do the morally, socially, and spiritually significant work of resisting the prevailing spirit of the age which tends toward reduction and reaction.

Most importantly, this book offers a philosophical and pedagogical foundation for approaching education as not merely a form of information delivery but of character formation. Not every teacher in every classroom setting is be able to implement the condensed curriculum of the catechisms suggested here. But every teacher in every classroom will be inspired by the pages that follow to fill and form their students' memories with words that are good, true, and beautiful.

Karen Swallow Prior, PhD
Liberty University

Introduction

When I was young, I was a thief. I stole many things, most of them quite petty. I never got caught. I took very few chances and only stole when I was confident I could get away with it. At some point around the time I turned twenty-one or twenty-two, I realized that other people owned things and had rights to those things, and that if I took those things without asking, I was clearly in the wrong. As an adolescent, the question I had always asked was, "Can I get away with this?" Only when I became an adult did I ask, "Should I get away with this?" The former question was purely practical, while the latter question was moral. Practical questions are not inconsequential to a good and virtuous life, but they don't often play a major role, and thus, as someone who was primarily concerned with practical questions, I had little interest in virtue.

I spent the first several years of my teaching career mainly asking practical questions on tests and quizzes. "When was Dante born?" is a practical question, or I supposed it was. I asked questions about the English Civil War and had students recapitulate dates of battles and names of lords. I asked for plot synopses, summaries of chapter two, or syntheses of the arguments presented in book six. While conducting class, however, I rarely asked practical questions, for my students were ambivalent about answering them. They might know the name of Henry VIII's second wife, but when I asked, few of them thought the question interesting enough to warrant a raised hand. Answering such questions was slavish work, and so someone else could take care of it. However, moral questions generally elicited a far more robust response. Questions like, "If we treat Victor Frankenstein as a negative example, what do we learn about living a satisfying life?" returned varied, insistent, and passionate responses.

Over the years, I realized that the answers to practical questions could be stolen, while the answers to moral questions could not. A student might write all the names in the Stuart line on the palm of his hand before a test, but if I asked students how Edmund Burke made them want to change the way they watched television, cheating wasn't really possible. They could use whatever resources they liked because genuine classicists believe that answering a moral question well means not positing an original answer but finding the most beautiful and most elegant answers which others have given.

I never stole anything worth keeping. Easy come, easy go, and so I tended to lose track of the things I stole. If those things were not worth spending time and effort to acquire, neither were they worth hanging on to. Bad money drives out good money, and the same is true of bad things and pointless knowledge. Stolen money disappears about as quickly as a crammed list of names and dates for a history test.

My tendency to steal began to fade around the time I began visiting art museums. The economy on which an art museum functions defies the need to steal. In 2004, while aimlessly wandering around downtown Chicago, I paid to enter the Art Institute and saw Gregory Crewdson's *Untitled (Ophelia)*, which I gazed at in unfeigned admiration for ten minutes. Even if I stole the photograph, I could not steal the encounter I had with it, which was sudden, transfixing, morose. The temple-like experience of the Chicago Art Institute, and then the High Museum of Art in Atlanta several years later, and finally the Metropolitan (but also the Frick, the Cloisters, and the Morgan) in New York, had a lingering and diffuse effect on what I thought education could be. My first trip to Manhattan was transformative, despite the fact that it involved no study, no quiz, and no "accountability for the material," so to speak. Overwhelming experiences are memorable in and of themselves.

What if class could be the same way? What if assessments could be the same way? What if class could not be stolen?

My continued ruminations on these trips, married with my chagrin for having wasted so much of my youth on vice, have finally become this little volume, which is a guidebook for helping teachers make their classes memorable, necessary, and transformative.

Joshua Gibbs
North Hall, Veritas School
Richmond, VA

What is not retained is not learned."

From one year to the next, high school students retain very little of what they are tested over. Ask a class of chemistry students, "How many of you could pass a biology exam you took last year?" and they will laugh. Ask a class of sophomore literature students, "How many of you could pass a freshman lit exam?" and they will merely smirk and cast furtive, knowing glances to one another, for they do not recall the names of minor characters, they cannot reconstruct the third act of *Hamlet*, and they do not remember whether Laertes was the son of Polonius, or Polonius the son of Laertes. Neither do they remember what a "synecdoche" is, or a "trope," or what the difference is between a simile and a metaphor.

Of course, six or seven months ago, they "knew" all these things; they all passed an exam on Shakespeare with flying colors. The students were given a review sheet for the exam which included a long list of terms and characters to know, as well as a half-dozen essay questions which might appear. Once the review sheet was passed out, each student dutifully sat on his bed in the evening, glossed his notes, perhaps made some flash cards, and stuffed as many facts and schemes into his head as would fit. Three days later, having taken the exam, the facts and schemes slowly disappeared from the mind of each student.

When a teacher asks a class of sophomores, "How many of you could pass a freshman literature exam?" there are several reasons why the students flash each other knowing glances. First, the students believe the teacher is expecting a positive, affirming response to the question. They believe this because they find their teachers a bit naïve, and who could blame them? After all, ever since seventh grade, their teachers have been asking them to "memorize" facts and lists which they all summarily forget as soon as they can. Students are not sure how their teachers have not picked up on this yet, for if their teachers knew how little they recalled, surely they would do things differently. Second, the students believe that in forgetting what they were tested over last year, they have gotten away with something, almost like a con or a scam. That students should feel triumph at forgetting, and not shame or fear, is perfectly reasonable, though, for the students do not believe that anything they are studying will be of value to them once they are grown. Thus, forgetting whether Polonius was the son of Laertes is actually the responsible thing to do. It is intellectual decluttering.

The teacher cannot blame the students for feeling clever at having forgotten so much, for the students have simply gamed a system which the teacher has ignorantly set up. The teacher himself is well-aware of how much from his own high school education has been lost. The teacher was required to learn lists of kings and emperors, the periodic table, the parts of a cell, timelines, thousands of terms and key words and definitions, and he recalls next to none of it. As a teacher, he regularly finds himself writing tests and quizzes which look like the tests he took in high school. He sometimes admits to himself that he recalls little of high school. Nonetheless, he blithely continues requiring his students to jump through arbitrarily constructed memorization hoops, for he doesn't know any other way of teaching or testing. From time to time, the teacher tries to convince himself that he is not wasting his students' time. He tells himself, "Some of these students may go on to be English majors, and the time they have spent memorizing the definition of 'simile' and 'synecdoche' will have been good preparation for later studies." This is specious reasoning, though, for the literature student who "memorizes" facts about *Hamlet*, Shakespeare, and poetic devices in high school nonetheless encounters the same material once more in college as though for the first time. What is more, college is by no means the place where the English major finally commits "synecdoche" to memory. The English major will be looking up definitions, facts, and the dates of Shakespeare's life for the next twenty years.

How Humans Memorize

Teachers would do well to consider how most things are memorized. At no place outside of a modern school (college, academy) are human beings *asked* to memorize anything. We *accidentally memorize* phone numbers, addresses, computer passwords, directions, lyrics to songs, the Nicene Creed, the Pledge of Allegiance, and volumes of information which pertains to our employment, and yet none of these things are committed to memory the way a sophomore history student "memorizes" the Stuart line. All these things are memorized by repetition. If a man really needs to remember something, he writes it down, and he refers over and over to what he has written until it becomes second nature. When a young man gets a job at a restaurant, his boss gives him the code for the alarm system and says, "Write this down." The young man writes it down, puts the number in his wallet, and for the next two weeks, every night, he pulls the number out to make sure he enters the code properly. After two weeks, he knows the number by heart. He knows the number by heart because *he needs to know it*, and he has learned the number through habitually using it. At no point does the young man sit on his bed and memorize the number from the scrap of paper where he jotted it down. There is no need. Besides, even if he were to commit the code to memory while laying on his bed, he would likely have the scrap of paper out the following night just to make sure he remembered it properly—especially if an alarm went off when the code was entered improperly.

Nearly everything a man memorizes is codified in his heart through habitual use. As a history and literature teacher, I know scores of facts off the top of my head. I know Dante's *Comedy* was finished in 1321. I know the Peace of Augsburg was signed in 1555. I know the King James Bible was finished in 1611. At some point in high school, I probably had to memorize these dates for a history test, and I may very well have gotten the questions on the exam right. However, after I graduated high school in 1999, I did not encounter these dates again for more than a decade, and thus they entirely departed from my mind. I did not simply *forget* these dates. It was as though I never knew them. If a man knows his anniversary is coming up but forgets and then is reminded of the fact on the day of, he says, "Ah, that's right! It's today!" However, by the time the average American hits his ten-year high school reunion, he has so thoroughly forgotten what he learned sophomore year that, were he to encounter the material again, he would not say, "That's right! Of course, the Peace of Augsburg was signed in 1555." He would say, "The Peace of what? I have no idea when it was signed. 4 BC? 1992? Last year?"

I encountered 1321, 1555, and 1611 for the second time around ten years after I graduated high school, and I only encountered them because I had begun teaching high school. At some point in the last fourteen years of teaching, I knew by heart that the Peace of Augsburg was signed in 1555, though I couldn't say when exactly I had the date memorized. For many years, I had to look the date up whenever I needed to know it, and the same is true of a hundred thousand other names and definitions. If I continue teaching great books for the next ten years, I will probably come to know Dante's birth year by heart, as well as the dates for the English Civil War, the Thirty Years' War, and the names of lesser demons in *Paradise Lost*. For now, when I need to know these things for a lecture or an article, I do what any reasonable person does. I look them up.

Nonetheless, a great many high school literature teachers— even self-professed classical teachers—are regularly handing out exams which are full of questions which require the student to "know" 1321, 1555, and 1611. In case you would like the inside story on such teachers, I don't mind telling you that many of them do not know these dates by heart either. They require their students to know certain names and dates from memory, but do not personally know the dates from memory. In my first several years teaching, I was just such a teacher. I did not know what education was for. I was a terrible hypocrite. By this point in my career, I have taught the *Divine Comedy* a dozen times and I have a daughter named Beatrice, but I still do not know the year Dante was born. Sometime in the 1260s or 1270s. Who cares? I do not ask the question glibly, but out of genuine intrigue. Knowing the exact year of his birth is not going to help me understand the paradoxical inscription which appears on the gates of Hell. Knowing the exact year will not help me better govern my soul like a king.

The Problem of Subjectivity

Young teachers are intimidated to ask questions on tests and quizzes which aim at moral formation, however, because such questions are thought subjective and students often complain they cannot study for such tests. Most students believe that "In what year was the *Comedy* finished?" is an objective question because liberal, conservative, Christian, and atheist would all agree the answer is 1321—but most students are wrong. The answer is objective, the question is not.

When the question, "In what year was the *Comedy* finished?" appears on a literature exam, it has been subjectively chosen by the teacher. "1321" must be the answer to the question, but the teacher is under no obligation to ask such a question. In asking the question, the teacher is subjectively determining that knowing the date the *Comedy* was finished has value. The teacher has chosen to incentivize knowing what year the *Comedy* was finished over many other questions which he might ask, like, "In the first canto of the *Inferno*, Dante knows heaven exists, but he does not truly want to go there. Why do you not want to go to heaven? Are your reasons more or less shallow than Dante's reasons?" Of course, the teacher has also determined that knowing the year the *Comedy* was finished is more valuable than knowing the year Dante began writing it, or knowing the year Dante was born, or the year Beatrice died. The teacher could also ask what century Dante was born, or what decade, or he might ask what day of the month Dante was born, or the day of the week. If the teacher believes it is more important to know the *Comedy* was finished in 1321 than to know the names of Dante's parents, he should be capable of explaining why. However, if the teacher is truly capable of making a case for the importance of knowing when the *Comedy* was finished, he has damned himself nonetheless, for he must also admit that his students will not remember the date the following year. We should ask, "Why are you not teaching the students important things in a manner they will recall in the future?" for the fact of the matter is that, two years later, none of the students will be able to guess the year of Dante's birth within a century in either direction. If the date is not important, students should not be asked to have it memorized for two weeks, and if the date is important, students should not have it memorized for a mere two weeks.

By What Standard?

Dates and names and definitions are rather easy to test over, which goes a long way in explaining the allure of dates and names. If a student claims on a test that Dante was born in 1854, the teacher can mark the answer wrong and not worry that the student (or, more significantly, his parents) will complain. The teacher can say, "I told the students what dates would be on the exam. This date was on the review sheet, and so it was fair game for the exam." Parents and students alike rarely balk at class time being frittered away with games, "study hall" periods (wherein the students flirt and gossip while the teacher grades a stack of papers), or videos being shown in class, but the matter of grades is deadly serious, and teachers know this. What is more, most parents and students are perfectly content for the teacher to ask convicting questions about moral development on a test provided the student ultimately gets an A; however, should an unusual essay prompt earn the student a C, the teacher will suddenly have half a dozen people asking, "By what standard?" Such scenarios are as common as daisies.

The use of a rubric will not help the teacher. Although rubrics offer the illusion of an objective evaluation, in the end a fallible and opinionated human being must decide whether young Brooklyn's essay "mostly failed" or "completely failed" to make a coherent argument (these are objective expressions which might appear on a rubric). Every classical school in the country has a rubric for grading essays which was crafted by some former employee. That rubric has been buried under a mountain of bureaucracy and left unconsulted for years. Rubrics are not like doorstops or can-openers. They are hard to use, ineffective, and inconvenient. I have several times fielded angry phone calls from fathers who insisted they had read their daughter's essay on Boethius and "thought it was pretty good," but also insisted the low grade young Piper received was not objectively supported by a preestablished and minutely explained set of criteria. A rookie teacher need only have one such argument with a parent before going back to "In what year did Dante finish the *Comedy*?"

Ours is a materialist culture, though, which means we overvalue objectivity and do not understand the necessity of subjectivity. A great many modern men confuse "subjective" and "arbitrary." An arbitrary thing has no cause, no nature. If a man finishes eating a steak and says, "That steak was delicious," he has made a subjective judgment. If he says, "That steak was sixteen dollars," he has made an objective judgment. If he says, "Steaks are saxophones, Dr. Isosceles," he has spoken arbitrarily. A subjective judgment wagers the worth of a thing, the goodness of a thing, not merely the substance of a thing, though worth is often based on substance. Objectively speaking, a diamond is a rock. Subjectively speaking, a diamond is expensive. Subjective judgments are not merely based on feeling, but on discernment, community, and circumstance, as well as experience and the poetic interpretation of experience. When I say subjective judgments are based on experience, I simply mean that the opinion of an expert matters far more than the opinion of a common man.

Be not deceived, all opinions are not equally meritorious. The opinion of a Michelin three-star chef on the subject of tomatoes matters far more than a twelve-year-old boy's judgment that "Tomatoes are gross." The well-trained chef has absorbed more of the world than the boy, and so his opinion has a greater stake in reality. Neither is the twelve-year-old responsible for the world, or even the world of food, and thus he has little to gain or lose in his opinion of tomatoes. Little has been given the boy, and little is required. A good school should thus aim to hire teachers whose opinions matter, teachers who have something on the line when they speak, and who only speak on matters about which they have a growing reputation. The good teacher also invests his time outside of class on matters which will help his students take him more seriously. The good teacher is morally obligated to like better movies than his students, listen to better music and read better books. He laughs at all attempts to "redeem and reclaim video games for Jesus Christ." The good teacher aims to be a great sage of subjectivity, not a master of objectivity.

In both England and the United States, the opinions of common people are rarely admissible in a court of law, but if a witness is admitted as an "expert witness," he may give all the opinions he likes, provided they are in the range of his expertise. Objectivity makes life possible, but subjectivity makes life livable and good. Raw potatoes might keep a man alive, but raw potatoes cannot delight his heart the way tartiflette will. Food, air, shelter, and clothing are material necessities, objective necessities, and our bodies could not survive without them; but subjective things serve the soul.

Ain't Life Subjectively Grand?

The beauty of Michelangelo's *Pietà* and the grandeur of Mozart's Requiem Mass are real and grounded in objective qualities of either work, but neither the beauty nor the grandeur can be touched, weighed, or measured, and in this sense, their glory is subjective. This does not mean their glory is illusory, for the grandeur of the Requiem Mass is not really up for debate. In fact, the subjective grandeur of the Requiem Mass has outlived many of the objective claims of scientists who lived at the same time as Mozart. The subjective judgments men make of beauty tend to be more lasting and more absolute than most objective claims about the world. Seven hundred years later, the world still attends to Dante's *Comedy*, even though every page of the book is shot through with Dante's geocentric beliefs. The beauty of Dante's poetry transcends his factual, material knowledge of astronomy. How many beliefs about the elements, minerals, medicine, and biology have we discarded since Michelangelo finished his *Pietà*? And yet the *Pietà* is still here. "The *Comedy* was finished in 1321" is an objective claim but is subject to revision, for it might be based on forged historical documents. Scientific formulas are objective, but they are subject to revision and refinement. New discoveries are more apt to change science, but no new discovery will change "Love thy enemies," or "As kingfishers catch fire, dragonflies draw flame," or the mesmerizing ambiguity of Mona Lisa's smile. The idea that objectivity is necessarily longer lasting or less transient than subjectivity is specious.

Taken side by side, the subjective beauty of a poem written this year is apt to outlive the objective claims of science or history made at the exact same time. Unlike science or history, beauty does not exist "to the best of our knowledge," while Pluto is a planet one week, but not the next, and then a planet once again come April. Had Newton not discovered his laws of motion, someone else could have. On the other hand, if Michelangelo had not carved his *Pietà*, no one else would have made it. In creating the *Pietà*, the sculptor Michelangelo made subjective claims about the human body which have survived well beyond objective claims made about the human body by many of Michelangelo's contemporaries.

I say this not to denigrate the hard sciences, but as a desperate attempt to reestablish the unique, unrepeatable, and irreplaceable worth of the subjective value of art. Despite the ways in which science is typically compared with art (in our materialist age), the power of science is that it is not absolute, but rather subject to endless improvement, while the power of beauty and philosophy and theology is absolute, for these things are not subject to refinement. "Love your enemies" brooks no edits. New evidence will not overthrow "He who has much, wants much," and Debussy's *La Mer* is not open to correction and revision based on recent discoveries about the sea.

But what has all this to do with tests and quizzes?

The subjective power of art and literature is often granted second-class status in modern academia, even in many classical schools, and treated as little more than an agreeable, attractive decoration which adorns the more real, more substantial economic power of STEM studies. Science and math are objective, which means they can be assessed objectively, and a student may commit sufficient hours of study to chemistry and biology so that he will be confident, prior to the exam, that he will ace it. On the other hand, no amount of preparation can guarantee the literature student a perfect score on an in-class essay, because the essay is not really correct or incorrect, but good or bad based on the subjective assessments of the teacher.

The Dangers of Pure Objectivity

If Wikipedia could ace your exams, you are not teaching human beings but machines. Most human beings will not do difficult things unless they are asked to. Unless the teacher asks his students to say interesting things, they will not. The teacher is free to incentivize whatever he likes. He may incentivize the ephemeral "memorization" of data, or he may incentivize profundity of thought. If the teacher requires students to say deep things and draw connections between things and ideas and philosophies and theologies and art and saints, his students might become interesting and virtuous human beings. Knowledge is merely *knowing that certain things are*, but wisdom is knowing *how the souls of things rhyme with each other*.

The student's task is to think, to ruminate, and so the student needs to learn that first impressions are worth very little in the classroom. The first impression requires no real contemplation, but is a reflexive, intuitive response to the world. First impressions are not without value in the world, but they should be worth very little in terms of testing, quizzing, essays, and grades. First impressions are often nothing more than common sense, but common sense should have no more value in the classroom than eating, breathing, or raising one's hand. The man who only runs until he is winded will not build stamina or distance, and the student who is never required to think beyond what comes naturally or easily will never develop the ability to see beyond appearances. "A fool gives full vent to his spirit, but a wise man quietly holds it back" (Prov. 29:11), Solomon teaches, and thus it is the work of an intellectual to not say the first thing which comes to mind. Neither does he say the second, third, fourth, fifth, sixth, seventh, eighth, or ninth thing which comes to mind. Having arrived at the ninth thing, he measures his thoughts again and goes back to the eighth thing, then the seventh thing. He refines the seventh thing by tempering it with the common sense of the first thing, and he uses the third thing as leaven. Then the intellectual speaks what is in his mind.

The intellectual believes that the first thing which comes to mind is rarely wrong, and yet it is often not best. If the first thing which came to mind was best, all men would be rich and fat and happy. However, there is a great disparity in the happiness of men, and the wise man has seen that fools usually act according to their first impressions, obey impulses, think little of consequences, and trust all appearances. The intellectual does not distrust first impressions or appearances, but neither does he act on first impressions when there is a lot on the line.

However, the fool responds to the wise man by saying the first thing which comes to mind. The fool is content that the wise man has never thought of the first thing simply because he has not said it. The fool despises the wise man for thinking too much and acting too little. The fool trusts appearances, believes the first thing he hears, and values his own opinion so highly that he never calls it into question. The fool believes that a man necessarily says everything he thinks (for the fool says everything he thinks), therefore, the man who believes something which is contrary to first impressions is too stupid to see the world for what it is.

When the wise man is finished speaking, he should not poll a crowd for first impressions. The wise man should teach with authority, and not submit his prudently articulated seventh impressions for the approval of a crowd unaccustomed to anything beyond a first or second impression. First impressions and seventh impressions are both opinion, but Welch's and wine are made of the same substance. Seventh impressions are heady and rich like cabernet, first impressions are sweet like juice. First impressions are the stuff of childhood, wine the stuff of maturity. If a teacher does not give his students the chance to work around to eighth and ninth impressions, he should not expect them to be able to think deeply, for deep thinking evidences time invested in a book. Any test on Dante's *Comedy* or Augustine's *Confessions* worth taking can only be completed by someone who has been ruminating on the book for many weeks.

A test is not merely an opportunity for the student to show what he has learned; a test should be a learning experience in itself. This means that it is not possible to cheat on a good test. A teacher is obliged to test his students in a manner similar to the way God tests men. A good test should be psychologically and theologically realistic. None of the tests which God gives in this life are closed-book, and all good Christians should either weep for or mock the man who brags at having overcome this or that trial "without ever cracking his Bible open." God sends us trials for our own edification, not to condemn us, for there is no trial given by God which cannot be overcome.

School is life, but school should also be an *homage* to life. Students should learn in the classroom in the same way they learn outside the classroom. I am thirty-seven and I have undergone many tests—tests of faith, tests of strength, tests of endurance. In some sense, those tests revealed to me what I was. In another sense, those tests made me what I am. I would not be the same person I am without having taken those tests, which is to say those tests were transformative. A test in which the student merely represents the sum total of what he has learned in class is neither transformative nor instructive. The student is the same whether he takes the test or not. A transformative test, a test which testifies to the sacramental nature of reality, is a live event, not a scrimmage. The student should be startlingly aware that he might write something shallow and trite, and shallowness is not morally neutral.

The ability to write and employ righteous tests, however, is dependent on a great deal of objectivity. The subjective beauty of Michelangelo's *Pietà* owes quite a lot to an objective knowledge of balance, proportion, marble, and tradition. My contention is not that objectivity has no value, but that teachers frequently overrate the importance of objectivity in what content they test on and how they incentivize higher grades. Further, the manner in which objective information is tested means it is rarely retained, and poor retention breeds contempt in students for their work and brings them to view school as arbitrary and silly. The silliness of school naturally brings students to think more highly of sports, friends, and popular culture: The lyrics to favorite songs are not easily forgotten, and the importance of sports does not depend on *remembering* sports, but in *doing* them. However, class is of little value in and of itself.

On the Divinity of Sports

Every student has had the demoralizing experience of missing a day of school, asking the teacher what was missed, and being given five minutes' worth of make-up work. Any sane person would judge a sixty-minute class which can be condensed into five minutes of make-up work to be a fifty-five-minute waste of time. Small wonder students take sports more seriously than class given that no one can cram an hour of basketball practice into ten minutes. It takes an hour to practice basketball for an hour. What is more, very few high school students expect to become professional basketball players or track stars, which means they do sports for the sake of sports and are not attempting to trade sports for something better.

When a math teacher explains the laws of geometry, he will occasionally have to answer the question, "When are we actually going to use this in the real world?" The question is a trick, though. Students ask this question to confirm the slavish nature of geometry work. No basketball player has ever been shown a diagram of a play and asked the coach, "When are we going to use a pick and roll in the real world?" Basketball players never ask about the real world when studying plays because the plays are good in and of themselves. So, too, the wine enthusiast does not ask about real-world application when being offered a cool glass of Riesling, even though drinking it will not help him pay the bills. As far as "use in the real world" is concerned, the things we *love* tend to be useless. God Himself is useless, for all things are used to reach God. The idea that God is useful is blasphemous, for it means He is a means to an end, in which case, that end is actually god.

The closer a thing is to God, the more useless it becomes. Pliers are useful and not particularly divine, as are glue, tacks, bricks, clothing, and lightbulbs. Money is about as useful as things get, and if Christ is to be believed in Matthew 19, the quicker a man abandons his money, the closer he gets to perfection. Sports are almost entirely useless, though, and so sports are divine. The more necessary history class is for success in the world, the less divine it becomes. If history class is about grades, scholarships, better jobs, and better paychecks, then history class is servile, inevitable, no less mundane than brushing your teeth. The less necessary basketball is, the more godlike, for it is the hobby of a free man, a noble, a man who is not purely governed by material needs and social obligations.

Many teachers suffer from the delusion that students will care deeply about a thing if that thing is shown to be necessary for success in their next lives as adults. In thirteen years of teaching, though, I have generally found teenage sympathies are nearly impenetrable by concerns for the future. This is no hard and fast law, but proverbially true. I cannot fault teenagers for this, for they have not yet taken possession of themselves. The law does not take them seriously, most teenagers serve no necessary material function in the family, and very few of them have yet developed a lifelong physical malady which the Almighty will use to remind them of their mortality. I was informed I had kidney disease in my high school days, but upon hearing it would not really affect me until my fifties, I nearly went away skipping, thinking, "Nothing is wrong with me at all!"

When a geometry teacher is asked what "real-world application" geometry will have, he will be tempted to show students a graph which displays all the professions which require a knowledge of geometry. In presenting the value of geometry as such, the teacher is guilelessly attempting to bring the heady realm of mathematics down to the practical and common world of laborers and bill payers. However, such graphs ultimately prove school is a means to an end and not an end in itself, for connecting geometry with the words "architect" and "civil engineer" more deeply establishes the connection between grades and money. Worse still, when students ask why they need to know geometry, many teachers are given to say, "You don't know what you'll be when you grow up. Maybe you'll be an architect; then you'll be glad you studied geometry in high school." Such claims make school out to be some kind of strange lottery, wherein many things are studied, most things are forgotten, and of the small portion of things actually remembered, most are still ultimately without value merely because they are not used to make money.

In brief, the good teacher must acknowledge the paradoxical fact that testing over content actually makes retaining content ifficult. The less content retained from one year to the r one month to next), the more pointless the class. The oncerned the teacher is with presenting content, the less necessary class becomes, for content is easily condensed. The more easily class is condensed, the less transformative the class, for the class will merely be a means to an end, not an end in itself. The good teacher gives his students time, space, and a reason to not be satisfied by first impressions. Objective facts never go beyond the superficial, for objective facts are concerned with material, not spirit. The good teacher, however, is ultimately concerned with the spirit.

CHAPTER TWO

Ceremony Is the Solution

A great many of the lamentations, fears, and frustrations expressed in the previous chapter slowly dawned on me over the first decade of my career as a teacher, and yet they all came into focus a few years ago when I led a class of medieval literature students to the Cloisters in Manhattan. We enrolled for a tour, and the first question the docent asked the class was, "When was the medieval era?" None of my students answered. The docent asked the question again, and stony silence followed once more. For the last eight months, this class had been immersed in the medieval era. They had studied late antiquity, Augustine, Boethius, and Charlemagne. They had read essays on the prominence of bishops after the collapse of the Roman empire, and the building of cathedrals which helped usher in the Renaissance. They had been quizzed on the dates of the medieval era earlier in the year and answered correctly. These students were not slackers, nor were they bored with their work. They were well-behaved, respectful, and well-mannered enough to be embarrassed (and not amused) that no one knew the answer to the docent's question. The dates of the medieval era had not merely slipped their minds, like a birthday or anniversary. When the docent finally gave them a range of years for the medieval era, they looked intrigued, as though this were their inauguration into such knowledge.

The trip occurred toward the end of the year, and so I had the entire summer to mull over their silence. My first thought was to try to make my medieval literature class more medieval in method, not just in content. What if my students were not only learning medieval content, but learning that content in a manner similar to the way medieval men would have learned it? To this end, I devised three rather straightforward ways in which my medieval literature class would take on a more medieval form.

Medieval Reforms

First, all written work would be saved. No medieval man would have written something down and then thrown it away. Vellum was too expensive for that, so I purchased cheap notebooks for my students in which all their work was submitted. Longer assignments could be typed and printed out, but the printouts had to be cut to size and taped into the notebooks. This meant I never misplaced their work, but their work was slowly collected all in one place. I could also look back over all the notes, comments, and grades which I had given as the year progressed. If, in February, I wrote, "You will have to redo your work if it is this messy again," at the top of a short essay prompt, come March, I could look back and see I had already cautioned a student about his penmanship, or remember to commend him for doing better. Second, I wrote a long and detailed rule of decorum for my classroom which borrowed from several monastic traditions. The first rule of decorum had nearly twenty items, and students copied the rule out by hand in their notebooks. However, it was the final medieval reform I enacted which has ultimately born the most fruit, and I would not hesitate to say the final reform has proven to be the single most significant and helpful development in my fourteen years as a teacher: I wrote a catechism for each of my classes and had my students recite it every day at the beginning of class.

The word "catechesis" simply means "oral instruction," and I conceived of each catechism I wrote as a series of questions and answers centered around the curriculum of the class. Every major work covered in class was somewhere referenced in the catechism, and the catechism was recited at the beginning of every class; thus, each individual class period began with the entire class year represented in microcosm. The catechism contained all the content from the class which I wanted my students to commit to memory, including long passages from our texts. In finalizing the questions and answers on a catechism, I admitted to myself that all content outside the catechism would likely be forgotten by the following year.

On the first day of class, I offered a lengthy apologia for the use of the catechism, much of which flows through the pages of this book. I knew I could not foist such a project upon them without an explanation, and I wanted the explanation to be honest, transparent, and philosophical. I began this apologia by asking them how much of the content they studied in previous years of school was still with them, and they laughed. We spent a moment discussing why so much was so quickly forgotten, but then I asked, "While you may have forgotten a great deal of what you have been tested over, I am also certain there are things you learned in the past which are still with you. What are those things?" After pondering the question a moment, they began to describe poems they remembered from years ago, then other lengthy pieces which they had performed in middle school. "I am not terribly concerned with how you memorized things you have long since forgotten, but how did you memorize the things which you still recall?" As they answered this question one by one, all their answers began with the same two words: *We all* . . . Simply put, everything they remembered years later had been memorized as a group.

Why We Remember

For years I had assumed the best way to emphasize the importance of certain material was to put it on a test and to tell students in advance that they would be tested over certain lists, names, dates, concepts, and themes. This was not necessarily a foolish assumption, for people naturally talk more often about things which are of greater importance, and when it comes time to write a test, should the teacher not ask his students to speak about important things as opposed to unimportant things? To be fair, I am sure the poems and lengthy pieces which my students remembered years later had initially been memorized for a grade. However, if a forty-line poem is memorized as a group, the fact everyone receives a grade for their recitation is relatively unimportant because there is really only one way to memorize something as a group, and that is to *recite it together*. What is more, groups of people do not randomly assemble. Rather, groups assemble at particular times and in particular places. This might seem obvious; however, the things which students memorize for a test and then forget are not studied at particular times and places. They are studied arbitrarily. The student who receives a study guide for a test might make flash cards and a

study sheet; however, he will sometimes look
classes, sometimes glance at it on the way to sch
peruse it between texts while lying on his bed,
in the moments before the exam. There is no c
and if the material is not significant enough to
will not encounter it much after the test has been taken.

On the other hand, the poems my students could recall years
later had been considered significant enough that their teachers
were willing to reorder their classes around that material, daily reciting the poem together until the words made an indeli-
ble impression upon their minds. Compare such a method for
memorization with the American history teacher who hands out
a copy of the Gettysburg Address, spends half an hour discussing it, and then tells a class of freshmen to have it memorized in
two weeks. Perhaps the teacher believes that attaching a grade
to the memorization of the Address is the best way of showing
students how important it is. If the Address is worth memorizing, is it worth saying every day in class for two months? If not,
why not? Some teachers might say the Address is worth memorizing, yet not worth spending so much class time on, but I find
this a rather straightforward contradiction. What is the point
of memorizing a thing if not to say it? If the teacher wants his
classroom to be *about the world*, he must use class time to show
students how to live. If the teacher wants students to speak Lincoln's words outside the classroom, they must speak Lincoln's
words inside the classroom.

The good classroom is an icon of the world, not an oasis from
the world. Students will not be convinced of the worth of the
Gettysburg Address unless the teacher is willing to suffer for it,
and one of the most significant losses which a teacher can un-
dertake is that of lost time. In fact, students do not learn what
the teacher tests on, they learn what he lavishes his minutes and

urs on. If a teacher will not spend his own time on something, he should not expect his students to do so. <u>The teacher is always modeling the use of time to his students.</u>

A Humanizing Ceremony

Of course, one should also not discount the psychological and spiritual gravity which weighs on words said *en masse*. When a formula is pronounced by a particular kind of person, in a particular place, at a set time, on a daily basis, what you have is not really a recitation, but a ceremony. The work performed in a ceremony establishes the identity of the people involved because ceremony is neither for amusement nor edification; ceremony is a way of being, a way of besting the vanity of life under the sun. To do a thing every day, at the same time, and according to the same customs is a little victory against time—time, which naturally destroys the body and corrupts the memory. Ceremonies pinch disparate times together and allow a man to know himself not as a series of accidents, not as a chaos of selves, but as a singular person who is uniquely responsible for his own actions. The greater the ceremony which attends a man's life, the better he knows himself and the more accurately he can judge himself.

On the last day of the school year, when students recite the sophomore or junior catechism for the last time, they gloss every canonical text and major point of study once more and view the year as one continuous whole. Before I began using catechisms, during the final quarter of the school year I regularly brought up books we read in the first quarter and suffered the demoralizing sigh of half the class before someone remarked, "Oh, that's right. We read that." But let us say that the first book a junior literature class covers is *Jane Eyre*, and that a morally weighty passage of the book is included in the catechism which is recited every day. The class never really finishes *Jane Eyre*. They might finish *reading* the book, but they are never *done* with it, for every class period opens with an invitation to incorporate Bronte's philosophy of human flourishing into the present day's reading from Burke, Rousseau, Dickens, or whomever. One of the great benefits of ceremonially performing a microcosm of the entire year on a daily basis is that the day's work is constantly set in its proper context. Nothing is arbitrary. Everyone always knows which way is up.

After explaining the way in which we would use the catechism, I made my students a promise which quelled their fear that the catechism would simply prove a hassle. I said, "All tests in this class will be open book and open note. I may give you the option of memorizing one passage of a book over another, but you will not have to "study" or "cram" in the conventional sense. I believe that, by the end of the year, you will have the entire catechism committed to memory, but I will never test you on it." This promise was greeted by my students with open-mouthed astonishment. Perhaps a few readers of this book are similarly astonished at such a promise, but a more thorough explanation awaits.

The First Five Minutes Problem

The practical benefits of the catechism were immediately discernible. In the many years before implementing the catechism, I had often tried to begin class with silence, contemplation, and perhaps a short writing exercise. I might write a provocative question on the board based on yesterday's class discussion and ask students to write for two or three minutes. This never worked, though. It is a truth universally acknowledged by high school teachers that the first five minutes of class are the least productive, for students are still buzzing with gossip and jokes from the hall, laughing, and catching one another's attention for one last word before having to commit themselves to some new intellectual task. There is, perhaps, no final cure for the assembly-line approach to teaching multiple subjects every day. An absurd amount of time is wasted every day transitioning between classes and classrooms, for even if the math classroom were adjacent to the history classroom, time would still be lost in readjusting to a different teacher, as well as a different set of expectations and rules. In truth, having students move to five different rooms over the course of a school day is like having a man sleep in five different beds every night. Why not have him sleep in one bed? Why wake him, and cart him from one bed to the next, bothering him to waste time, once again, trying to fall asleep? Similarly, why not have six weeks of literature class all day, then six weeks of history class, then six weeks of biology class, and so forth? Consider for a moment how little time would be lost walking across campus, and how little time would be wasted getting students to mentally switch gears between one subject and the next. Further, having many teachers over the course of a single day tempts students to try to get away with more, for every teacher enforces the rules differently. One teacher cares about the dress code and the next does not. One teacher cares about eating in class, the next does not. The student who is worried about getting away with something is not paying attention in class. I do not believe modern schools, even classical schools, will ever break themselves of the assembly-line format for classes. Nonetheless, the good teacher must try to account for the general worthlessness of the first five minutes of class after all. They make up nearly 10 percent of his school year.

The problems I always encountered when I began class with a short writing exercise were manifold. First, I could not always think of a very interesting or worthwhile question to ask. Second, if the question were really worth answering, it also required a few minutes to think over. No student could begin writing cold and say anything of value. Third, telling students who are still jittery with hall freedom to sit quietly and think for a few minutes is pointless because they need to be given something to *do*, not merely something to *think about*. Fourth, assuming the students were quiet and thoughtful for three or four minutes before beginning to write, I did not have enough time to look at sixty short essays every day, and the students knew this. Fifth, few high school students are mature enough to profitably use their time writing something they know no one will ever read. Hence, every September I resolved to daily begin class with a thoughtful question on the board, and by November, I had generally recognized my plan had collapsed into a farce.

Practical Benefits of Ceremony

The catechisms I write for my classes take around seven minutes to say in full (which seems like an egregiously long time if we labor under the delusion that the first several minutes of class are usually productive). Students should stand to recite the catechism. My students handwrite a copy of the catechism in their notebooks, and when they recite the catechism, they hold it open like a songbook, so they can project. The recitation is not busy work I give the students, for I recite the catechism myself, and I speak loudly with a good clip: not fast, but faster than I would read a book aloud. Students are sometimes tempted to lay the catechism open on their desks, but I insist they have their notebooks in hand. Over the first month of recitations, the time needed to say the catechism in full will quickly drop as the class becomes accustomed to the invisible rhythm of the words, developing cadences and points of emphasis. By the time the daily recitation is over, my students are winded. Speaking at a good volume and a good speed for seven straight minutes is a little exhausting, and when the recitation finishes, students are ready to sit down and be quiet—a fact which nearly justifies the use of the catechism in itself. How many high school teachers attempt to begin a lecture or discussion with students who are still itching to stand and chat?

After the recitation, when the teacher initiates discussion of the daily reading, he is not trying to get something *started*, but *continuing* something which the class has collectively begun. How much better to pose the day's first provocative question about Burke or Rousseau to a class which is already involved in intellection, has already spoken elegant things, and is already *physically involved* with the material? Use a catechism and the quiet boy who never talks in other classes will pronounce more brilliant words in just the first seven minutes of one period than he will say all year in classes which do not use a catechism. Granted, speaking in a group is quite different than speaking alone, on a stage, and yet I believe there is also some mysterious worth in the physical labor of saying true, good, and beautiful things. A man need not exercise by himself in order to personally grow strong, for soldiers train in groups, run in groups, do situps in groups; a single soldier does not fail to become fit because he works out with a hundred others. The passages from canonical texts included in the catechism are often not straightforward chunks of prose, but elaborate, twisting sentences which slowly disclose their meaning over the year. Thus, class begins with students going through the motions of greatness.

I am now in my third year using catechisms, and while I would not claim that my students have learned to love catechisms, they have quickly accepted the daily recitations as part of the furniture of the classroom. Dostoyevsky claimed that a human being was a creature who could get accustomed to anything, and after a month of recitations, students have largely forgotten how class used to begin.

Many of the benefits of the catechism which I have described up to this point merely concern crowd control, and yet, in the final months of the school year, when students have slowly committed the catechism to heart, they naturally begin to employ it of their own free will. Ideas, turns of phrase, and facts which students have daily recited begin showing up on their essays and in class discussions. This is what taking possession of a text looks like, if you prefer such language, but I would rather say this is what genuine surrender and submission to a text looks like. Having recited Edmund Burke's definition of human society a hundred times, or *Jane Eyre*'s final stand against Rochester's advances, or St. Paul's sermon to the epicureans and stoics, or Satan's barrage of reasons why Eve should eat the fruit, the student slowly comes to *possess* the text, not merely approve of it from a distance. In the final quarter of the school year, I find my students begin quoting from the catechism in tests and essays. The catechism slips as easily into their arguments and explanations as allusions to films or lines from popular songs. Many students do not even place quotation marks around quoted passages, but reference canonical words as though personally familiar with the authors. When students can quote from canonical texts in class with the same kind of ease and familiarity with which they quote from songs and movies when talking to their friends— this is not just learning, this is paideia.

Why Come to Class? What Is Class?

In the last few years, I have written several articles for the CiRCE

Institute on classroom catechisms, and I have lectured on their use for the Society of Classical Learning and for ClassicalU. In this time I have met several dozen people at conferences who have described their own use of a catechism. Those teachers who are most happy with it, and most convinced of its worth, have not tried to skimp on the time they commit to daily recitations. On the other hand, those who report only mild success say they use a catechism "once a week," or that their own catechisms are much shorter than the kind I recommend. So, too, some readers of this book may be tempted to write a three-minute catechism for their own classes to save time; however, it is unlikely the short catechism will reference all the significant material from the curriculum. Neither is the short catechism all that imposing, and students will not be inclined to respect something quick and perfunctory. The shorter the catechism, the less of an accomplishment it is.

However, when class begins with a seven-minute recital of canonical texts, by the time class discussion starts later, every student has already performed substantial intellectual work. Productive discussion simply does not take place in the first ten minutes of class, and cold-opening the class with a provocative question is almost always a non-starter. Students are not ready to speak sixty seconds after they walk into class. Rather, they need to be slowly reminded of who they are, what they are doing, and why they are doing it. Thus, regardless of the class, every catechism begins with the same eight questions:

Gentlemen, what are you?
I am a king, for I rule myself.

Ladies, what are you?
I am a queen, for I rule myself.

What does it mean to rule yourself?
I am free to do good. I am not the slave of my desires.

Who has made you kings and queens?
Those who are led by the Spirit of God are the children of God. The Spirit you received does not make you slaves, so that you live in fear again; rather, the Spirit you received brought about your adoption to sonship. And by Him we cry, "Abba, Father." The Spirit Himself testifies with our spirit that we are God's children. Now if we are children, then we are heirs—heirs of God and co-heirs with Christ, if indeed we share in His sufferings in order that we may also share in His glory. I consider that our present sufferings are not worth comparing with the glory that will be revealed in us. For the creation waits in eager expectation for the children of God to be revealed. For the creation was subjected to frustration, not by its own choice, but by the will of the one who subjected it, in hope that the creation itself will be liberated from its bondage to decay and brought into the freedom and glory of the children of God.
(From Rom. 8:14-21)

What is the bondage to decay?
The vices are pride, avarice, lust, envy, gluttony, anger, sloth.

What does it mean to be human?
The virtues are faith, hope, love, wisdom, justice, courage, temperance.

Why should we seek virtue?
St. James asks, What does it profit, my brethren, if some-

one says he has faith but does not have works? Can faith save him? If a brother or sister is naked and destitute of daily food, and one of you says to them, "Depart in peace, be warmed and filled," but you do not give them the things which are needed for the body, what does it profit? Thus also faith by itself, if it does not have works, is dead. But someone will say, "You have faith, and I have works." Show me your faith without your works, and I will show you my faith by my works. You believe that there is one God. You do well. Even the demons believe—and tremble! But do you want to know, O foolish man, that faith without works is dead? Was not Abraham our father justified by works when he offered Isaac his son on the altar? Do you see that faith was working together with his works, and by works faith was made perfect? And the Scripture was fulfilled which says, "Abraham believed God, and it was accounted to him for righteousness." And he was called the friend of God. You see then that a man is justified by works, and not by faith only. Likewise, was not Rahab the harlot also justified by works when she received the messengers and sent them out another way? For as the body without the spirit is dead, so faith without works is dead also.

The catechism is, quite simply, other people's words—the words of wise men, sage women, saints, and authors of Scripture. Class opens with the recitation of wise men's words because their words matter more than ours. We have not convened to judge the ancients, but to be judged by them; we have not gathered to speak our minds, but to have our minds formed by the Western canon. The classical classroom is not a focus group on old books, but a nest, a garden, a forge, a crucible, an ark. The use of the catechism begins to dispel the myth that school is a place for self-actualization, self-discovery, self-improvement, and self-expression. Rather, a classical education is chiefly concerned with self-denial, self-effacement, and self-rule. No basic truth about classical education is more easily and quickly forgotten, for a great many literature teachers labor under the delusion that discussion is good for its own sake, and that a lively classroom is necessarily a productive classroom.

I am eager to not be misunderstood, for I long to teach my students the art of good conversation and to show them how to follow a conversation wherever it wants to go. What is more, if the teacher would show his students how to be good listeners, he must listen, which means he must ask them difficult, vexing questions and allow them to slowly and painfully sort out the truth. All this said, the excellence of a classroom cannot be measured by volume. The classroom is not exempt from Christ's teaching that "on the day of judgement people will give account for every careless word they speak," or from Solomon's teaching that "when words are many, transgression is not lacking, but whoever restrains his lips is prudent" (Prov. 10:19). Upon receiving the news that she would bear the Christ, Mary was first silent, and then sang a meticulously composed work of theology.

In a society where people are encouraged to constantly, instantly share their thoughts on every little thing which happens, the daily recitation of a catechism is a powerful call to be quick to listen and slow to speak. Students will recite the canon for months and never be asked to comment on what they are saying. On the other hand, I regularly hear of ninth graders beginning Bible studies, and, when I ask who is going to lead the study, a certain fourteen-year-old boy is named. The only quality which guarantees this boy's competence to interpret the book of Galatians is his "love of the Lord," which often means he is friendly and extraverted. If you have ever eavesdropped on such a Bible study, you know that two minutes is spent reading a single chapter of an epistle, and then thirty minutes is spent guessing its meaning. The leader of the Bible study typically thanks and praises anyone who says anything at all because, like a rookie teacher, he needs someone to cover over embarrassing silence. When I hear that another such Bible study is in the works, I tell students, "Your intention to honor the Lord by reading His Word is good. Keep in mind, though, that you all regularly report how rarely you read your Bibles. Instead of reading just one chapter and then saying what you think it means, why not spend all the time you have reading the Bible aloud? For your own part, just say 'Amen' when your time is up." I am yet to have anyone take me up on this offer.

I do not write this to shame these students, because they are genuinely baffled by my suggestion. They have been raised like ancient Romans to believe that virtue resides primarily in public speaking, or else in the contemporary American virtues of "getting involved," or "changing the world," or "speaking your mind."

Because the news cycle devours every story and every character it produces with blistering rapidity, a man comes to believe that unless he voices his opinion about a matter now, he will never say anything of value about it. By the time he has contemplated a matter, taken a thorough inventory of his knowledge of the subject, worked his own thoughts down to an eighth or ninth impression, then dialed back his opinion to obey the dictates of temperance and elegance, the issue has already been forgotten about for a year. Wit, force, and passion have thus taken the place of depth and precision in public discourse. However, when the students hear on the first day of class that they will be reciting Burke and St. Paul and John Milton every day for the next nine months, time takes on new meaning and presents a dazzling, perhaps vertiginous range of possibilities.

Repetition and Silence

Over the last ten years, I have published more than one hundred film reviews online, though I have lately given up such writing because I find it too stressful and unprofitable. As the editor of FilmFisher, I found that people were only willing to read reviews of films that had just been released, or which had been released long ago. Any film released between two weeks and twenty years back went untouched. While I was the editor, I took up the habit of seeing a new film in the theater on Friday night, writing the review on Saturday, and publishing the review on Sunday. On such a schedule, there was little time to ruminate on the film, consider the plot, themes, vision of the director or screenwriter. Often enough, reviews of new films are little more than a chance for the critic to be clever. Nine times out of ten, a hastily written review of a new film can tell the reader if the film is worth seeing, but cannot provide a compelling framework for considering the film or proffer an arresting series of questions which open the film up for deeper consideration. For this reason, a great many reviews of new films contain little analysis or interpretation, but rather recapitulate the most fashionable dogmas of the zeitgeist and then indicate whether the film is a faithful son of our epoch or not. For films which deal with race, gender, marriage, or war, one often gets the impression the review was written months ago on the basis of the preview alone.

Around the time I began writing for FilmFisher, I also began writing essays for the CiRCE Institute on a variety of issues concerning classical education. The more time I spent writing about Dante and Augustine, the less satisfying I found film reviews. On a single viewing, and a single afternoon to think it over, I was not able to get below the surface of a film, and a great many films were little more than surface. It was not until my third or fourth time through the *Divine Comedy* that I had any opinions about it which were worth sharing, and most new films are barely worth seeing once, let alone three times. Honestly, what is there that really needs to be said about the latest remake of *Godzilla*? But ours is a culture which has incentivized hasty and witty judgments, and the teacher must establish the classroom as a refuge for those afflicted by the tyranny of needing to find something clever to say. While the recitation of a catechism involves speaking, it is paradoxical speaking, for it is also silence—a slowly accruing silence. Pagans repeat their prayers because their gods have thick skulls, and Christians repeat their prayers because they have thick skulls. Pagans believe they will be heard for their many words, but Christians believe they themselves will hear for their many words—and they will hear because they are silent, but God is speaking through them. Repetition clears the path from distractions.

The Classroom Is Holy, Nearly Holy

The classroom which exists primarily so students have a place to share their thoughts is neither classical nor worthy of the title "classroom." The nearest analogue of the classroom is the nave of a church, and the nearest analogue to the lecture is the sermon. If the minister of the Gospel can achieve real silence between the sentences of his sermon, he has accomplished something praiseworthy. However, the classroom does not exist so the teacher can share his thoughts, for the teacher is obligated to the same holy silence before the Western canon as are his students. As the minister to the Gospel, the teacher to his text. The Western canon is the sacrament of education, and must be administered by a vetted, worthy custodian. When the teacher of virtue puts a canonical text into the hand of the student, the teacher is necessarily saying:

This book is from your people. I am not giving you this book on my own. I represent the dead. The dead have told me what they want for you. I am an intermediary between you and the dead, between you and the past. You are lost because you do not know the past. You do not know why you are here, what you are supposed to do, or who you are. I am here to help you. The dead are here to help you.

The world is a very difficult place, but we have figured out a few things. The world devours and destroys most things, and almost nothing lasts and almost nothing conquers time. But this Book is one of the things which has lasted.

You will not like this Book. Things which people do not like—those things last. The things people like—those things do not last. You will be tempted to cling to the things you like and to say, "These things will last. I like them. Everyone likes them. Why would they not last?" But do not say that anything will last until it has lasted—saying that a thing will last before it has lasted is the great academic heresy. To say anything will last which has not lasted is treason against the things which have lasted. We are only men and we do not know the future. This Book that I am putting into your hands has lasted, though. You will not like it. And then, you will love it.

I am not giving you this Book because it is excellent. Excellent books do not last. I am giving you this Book because it is divine. The only way of discerning if a thing is divine is if

it dies and then returns from the dead. Death is human, re-
turn from death divine. The thing which returns to us from
the dead is not only divine but makes ready the human for
the divine. The man who wrote this Book is dead, and yet
he lives on. No one alive today has ever seen the man who
wrote this Book, and yet he commands us from the grave.
We listen to him because we do not like the things he says,
and we do not like the things he says because he says true
things, and we are not yet true men.

We are not here to judge this Book. We are here to be judged
by this Book.

When the person called *teacher* stands in the place
called *school* and gives the thing called *book* to the person
called *student*, no one is free to say and do as he pleases. When
the teacher gives a book to a student outside the classroom, the
rules are far more lax. When the student gives a book to a student inside the classroom, he is basically free. But the conver-
gence of these four things—the teacher, the school, the book,
the student—invokes a timeless ceremony, drafts on a timeless
power, and invisibly calls forth a separate and higher reality.

The classroom is something just less than sacred, but it is
something more than secular. The teacher is wise to err on the
side of the sacred. If the classroom is not sacred, it is Kmart. The
content of the catechism comes to the student in the form of a
catechism for this very reason. The teacher is the master of the
classroom precisely because he is obedient to the masters of the
canon. The minister of the Gospel is not allowed to say whatever
he wants, but must minister the Gospel. The teacher of classics is
the minister of the Western canon.

Classical Curriculum, Unclassical School

Using a classical curriculum does not necessarily make a school classical any more than using pagan curriculum makes a school pagan. Julian the Apostate forbade Christian schools of the fourth century from teaching pagan literature because he knew very well what Christians were doing with Homer and Virgil, and it was not honoring to the gods. So, too, the fact that a Christian school teaches Latin, logic, rhetoric, the *Odyssey*, and the *Aeneid* means little in itself, for it is possible to keep all the right books around and still do nothing more than inflate egos, worship the zeitgeist, and prepare students for quick, easy apostasy in college. Teachers are complicit in the cult of self-affirmation whenever they read long passages of classic literature aloud in class only to ask a room full of fourteen-year-olds, "So, what do you think?" as though the answer truly mattered. The teacher may assign as many classical texts as he likes, but unless the teacher presents the texts as authorities over himself, neither will his students accept the texts as authoritative. If the texts do not have authority over the students, then it does not matter if the teacher passes out copies of *The Pilgrim's Progress* or *Your Best Life Now*, for everything is merely grist for the ego.

However, the teacher who opens class with the recitation of passages from the canon does so as a testimony that he is not a proselytizer or soapboxer. The teacher recites the catechism along with his students in homage to Christ, who declared, "I have not spoken on my own authority, but the Father who sent me has given me a commandment—what to say and what to speak" (John 12:49). Neither does the classical teacher speak on his own authority, but only what the conciliar imperatives of the canon have decreed he speak. The catechism is not only a microcosm of the curriculum, for the daily recitation of catechism is an icon of the curriculum's jurisdiction over the classroom. In the same way the court rises when the judge enters, the class rises when the canon enters the classroom. Only this kind of honor can save the canon from becoming just another film, another song, another video that warrants nothing more than a hot take from a listless audience which is only willing to reward what is sexy and amusing with a sudden burst of attention and ad revenue.

By the end of the school year, students will have recited the catechism more than one hundred times. When assembling the catechism, teachers should be careful to include passages from classic texts which can sustain this much attention. While teachers may be tempted to stock their catechisms with straightforward passages which convey easily discernible messages and truths, such passages will not slowly unveil their secrets to students over the course of the year. Contemporary readers have little exposure to literature which repays multiple reads. We read for plot and for comprehension, but not for contemplation. Classic literature, on the other hand, is handed down with the expectation of multiple readings. If students have little respect for books on the whole, it is (in part) due to the fact that most contemporary works are not worth a second look but can be wholly absorbed with a cursory encounter. In a perfect world, there would be time enough for students to read *Paradise Lost* during freshman year, then again come senior year. I have occasionally heard literature teachers daydream of just how profitable it would be to turn senior year into a review of the best books from the previous five years—the fact that most high schools do not teach any great work for a second time is truly lamentable, for it sends students the message that the academy is mainly interested in acquainting students with great books. If Heraclitus was

right, and a man can not enter the same rive
some books which are not read the first tim
maiden voyage, *Frankenstein* is not yet fully *I*
that perfect world comes, though, teachers (
dents a taste of it with a catechism wherein th
enigmatic, most poignant passages of classic ......
over daily.

No Grades

I will happily grant that some benefits of a daily catechism are
nothing more than subtle forms of crowd control. However,
the greatest ideological coup of the catechism is the instilling
of so much content, the watermarking of such deep form, and
the allowance for so much contemplation *without ever assigning
a grade*. All the blessings of the catechism come to the student
apart from the compulsion and threat inherently bound up in
the possibility of failure. If teachers are disheartened with students who seem incapable of recognizing the value of education
apart from transcripts and scholarships, they must offer students
something of greater worth which is free and ungraded. However, teachers cannot merely tell students that virtue is more
important than grades, and then order and govern their classes
according to graded assessments. Students do not need reasons
to care about something other than grades. They need ways to
care about something other than grades.

CHAPTER THREE

Sample Catechisms

The first seven questions of every catechism I employ are always the same and do not depend on the grade or class. These seven questions constitute a précis for the whole project of classical Christian education. Following the précis, though, each catechism should proceed into the most morally, philosophically, and theologically rich content contained in the curriculum of any given class. When choosing this content, teachers should consider the struggles which are particular to the teenage years, even while they expect students to remember the catechism beyond high school. When a young man is tempted to sleep with his girlfriend, mentally recalling every name and date from the Stuart line will probably not help him remain chaste. Besides, if he really needs to know the Stuart line at any point later in his life, he should have sufficient time to look it up at his leisure. However, in the moment of temptation, a young man is not likely to Google "moral things to remember when you are tempted."

The teacher crafts the catechism hoping his students will recall every question in the midst of their trials. As he compiles the catechism, the good teacher must ask himself, at least once, "If, at some point in their lives, my students were each put in solitary confinement for a year, would there be enough in this catechism to keep them sane?"

At the same time, the catechism should not merely be a sermon about piety broken up over two dozen questions. The catechism for a medieval history class should give a fair synthesis of significant medieval beliefs, fears, and convictions, in addition to providing students with a call to piety and high moral conduct. The themes which the teacher returns to on a daily or weekly basis should appear in the catechism in their most condensed forms—this is true whether the catechism is written for a history class, a literature class, or an algebra class. No matter the curriculum, a catechism should prove a delicate balancing act for the teacher, wherein pastoral concerns, poetic interests, beautiful prose, and the elegance of Scripture are properly proportioned and ordered.

The Medieval Humanities Catechism

1. Why did St. Francis practice asceticism?

It is the highest and holiest of the paradoxes that the man who really knows he cannot pay his debt will be forever paying it. He will be forever giving back what he cannot give back and cannot be expected to give back. He will be always throwing things away into a bottomless pit of unfathomable thanks. Men who think they are too modern to understand this are in fact too mean to understand it; we are most of us too mean to practice it. We are not generous enough to be ascetics; one might almost say not genial enough to be ascetics. A man must have magnanimity of surrender, of which he commonly only catches a glimpse in love, like a glimpse of our lost Eden.

(From St. Francis of Assisi *by G.K. Chesterton)*

2. What did Boethius teach about the good life?

No man is rich who shakes and groans, convinced that he needs more (26). No man is so completely happy that something somewhere does not clash with his condition (30). Remember, too, that all the most happy men are over-sensitive. They have never experienced adversity and so unless everything obeys their slightest whim they are prostrated by every minor upset. So nothing is miserable except when you think it so, and vice versa, all luck is good luck to the man who bears it with equanimity (31). The more varied your possessions, the more help you need to protect them, and the old saying is proved correct, he who hath much wants much (35). Decide to lead a life of pleasure, and there will be no one who will not reject you with scorn as the slave of that most worthless and brittle master, the human body (60).

(From The Consolation of Philosophy *by Boethius)*

3. What does a good man suffer for the Lord?

According to Roland, "A man should suffer greatly for his lord, endure both biting cold and sweltering heat and sacrifice for him both flesh and blood."

(From The Song of Roland*)*

4. What poem is inscribed on the gates of hell?

I am the way into the city of woe,
I am the way into eternal pain,
I am the way to go among the lost.

Justice caused my high architect to move,
Divine omnipotence created me,
The highest wisdom, and the primal love.

Before me there were no created things
But those that last forever—as do I.
Abandon all hope you who enter here.

(From Mark Musa's translation of The Divine Comedy *by Dante)*

5. What does Dante teach about wasting our lives away in petty amusements?

Put off this sloth, for shame!
Sitting on feather-pillows, lying reclined
Beneath the blanket is no way to fame—
Fame, without which man's life wastes out of mind,
Leaving on earth no more memorial
Than foam in water or smoke upon the wind.

(From Mark Musa's translation of The Divine Comedy *by Dante)*

6. How did medieval Christians believe heaven and earth were connected?

The worshipping community here on earth was an outlying

colony, its prayer a distant echo of the perfect and unceasing praise offered to God in heaven by his angels and his saints. It was especially in its worship that the apparent distance between the earthly and heavenly community was bridged. Angels hovered around the eucharistic altar and carried the congregation's self-offering to the throne of God, bringing back his blessing. Angels also attended their eating and their drinking. At the center of this familiarity of human and divine was the assurance of being linked with a community which stood in God's direct, face-to-face presence. The saints were God's friends, but they also remained men's kin. Together with them, the whole community was in God's presence. The divine was always there, waiting like lightning to break through the cloud, to be earthed by the conduction of worship, of the altar, the church building, the saint, alive or dead.

(From *"From Rome to the Barbarian Kingdoms (330—700)"* by *Robert Markus in* The Oxford Illustrated History of Mankind, *edited by John McManners)*

7. The Medieval Timeline

313: The Edict of Milan legalizes Christianity.

325: The Council of Nicea confirms the dogma of the Trinity. The Medieval Era: 590 AD - 1440 AD

590: Gregory the Great becomes Pope; the medieval era begins.

622: The Hijra: Muhammad and his followers flee Mecca for Medina.

637: Jerusalem is conquered by Islamic forces.

800: Charlemagne is crowned Holy Roman Emperor by Pope Leo III.

843: The Treaty of Verdun splits the Carolingian Empire into West Francia, Lotharingia, and East Francia.

1054: Separation of Eastern and Western Churches

1095: Pope Urban II calls for a crusade to retake the Holy Land at the Council of Clermont.

1124: The great cathedral-building work of Europe has begun; the city replaces the feudal farm as the organizing principle of society.

1321: The Divine Comedy *is finished; the Italian Renaissance has begun.*

1440: Johannes Gutenberg develops the printing press; the modern era begins.

1453: The Ottomans overtake Byzantium, and the French defeat the English in the Hundred Years' War.

The Early Modern European Humanities Catechism

1. What is temptation and what is virtue?

I care for myself. The more solitary, the more friendless, the more unsustained I am, the more I will respect myself. I will keep the law given by God; sanctioned by man. I will hold to the principles received by me when I was sane, and not mad—as I am now. Laws and principles are not for the times when there is no temptation: they are for such moments as this, when body and soul rise in mutiny against their rigour; stringent are they; inviolate they shall be. If at my individual convenience I might break them, what would be their worth? They have a worth—so I have always believed; and if I cannot believe it now, it is because I am insane—quite insane: with my veins running fire, and my heart beating faster than I can count its throbs. Preconceived opinions, foregone determinations, are all I have at this hour to stand by: there I plant my foot.

(From Jane Eyre *by Charlotte Bronte)*

2. What is human society?

According to Edmund Burke, "... society is a partnership in all science; a partnership in all art; a partnership in every virtue, and in all perfection. As the ends of such a partnership cannot be obtained in many generations, it becomes a partnership not only between those who are living, but between those who are living, those who are dead, and those who are to be born. Each contract of each particular state is but a clause in the great primaeval contract of eternal society, linking the lower with the

higher natures, connecting the visible and invisible world, ac-
cording to a fixed compact sanctioned by the inviolable oath
which holds all physical and all moral natures, each in their
appointed place."

(*From* Reflections on the Revolution in France *by Edmund Burke*)

3. What are the defining features of the modern era?

Modernity aims to achieve its goals by erecting walls and
boundaries that will keep the world neatly divided and under
control. The wall of separation between religion and politics
will save politics from irrational passion. For moderns, distin-
guishing "us" from "them" is thus both temporal and spatial:
temporal because it distinguishes sharply between the present
and the past, spatial because it distinguishes sharply between
those who are up to date and those who are mired in a past
that moderns have transcended. We moderns organize our-
selves into rationally constituted nations; they are organized
by irrational blood-bound tribes. We recognize the difference
between religion and politics; they confuse the two. We separate
fine arts from daily life; with them arts and life are commingled.
We believe in equality and freedom; their lives are dominated
by hierarchy and slavery. We are rational; they are irrational.
Above all, the modern theory of progress rests on the notion that
we know nature as it truly is and thus have the ability to control
nature in the ways they never imagined.

(*From* Solomon Among the Postermoderns *by Peter Leithart*)

4. What is the Enlightened ethos?

Enlightenment is man's emergence from his self-imposed immaturity. Immaturity is the inability to use one's own understanding without another's guidance. This immaturity is self-imposed if its cause lies not in lack of understanding but in indecision and lack of courage to use one's own mind without another's guidance. Dare to know! "Have the courage to use your own understanding" is therefore the motto of the Enlightenment.

(From "What is Enlightenment?" by Immanuel Kant)

5. What is the conservative ethos?

Conservatism starts from a sentiment that good things are easily destroyed, but not easily created. This is especially true of the good things that come to us as collective assets: peace, freedom, law, civility, public spirit, the security of property and family life, in all of which we depend on the cooperation of others while having no means singlehandedly to obtain it. In respect of such things, the work of destruction is quick, easy and exhilarating; the work of creation slow, laborious and dull.

(From How to Be a Conservative *by Roger Scruton)*

6. Why does Satan tell Eve she should eat the forbidden fruit?

ye shall not die:
How should you? by the fruit? it gives you life
To knowledge; by the threatener? look on me,
Me, who have touched and tasted; yet both live,
And life more perfect have attained than Fate

Meant me, by venturing higher than my lot.
Shall that be shut to Man, which to the Beast
Is open? or will God incense his ire
For such a petty trespass? and not praise
Rather your dauntless virtue, whom the pain
Of death denounced, whatever thing death be,
Deterred not from achieving what might lead
To happier life, knowledge of good and evil;
Of good, how just? of evil, if what is evil
Be real, why not known, since easier shunned?
God therefore cannot hurt ye, and be just;
Not just, not God; not feared then, nor obeyed:
Your fear itself of death removes the fear.
Why then was this forbid? Why, but to awe;
Why, but to keep ye low and ignorant,
His worshippers? He knows that in the day
Ye eat thereof, your eyes that seem so clear,
Yet are but dim, shall perfectly be then
Opened and cleared, and ye shall be as Gods,
Knowing both good and evil, as they know.
That ye shall be as Gods, since I as Man,
Internal Man, is but proportion meet;
I, of brute, human; ye, of human, Gods.
So ye shall die perhaps, by putting off
Human, to put on Gods; death to be wished,
Though threatened, which no worse than this can bring.
And what are Gods, that Man may not become
As they, participating God-like food?
The Gods are first, and that advantage use
On our belief, that all from them proceeds:
I question it; for this fair earth I see,
Warmed by the sun, producing every kind;

Them, nothing: if they all things, who enclosed
Knowledge of good and evil in this tree,
That who so eats thereof, forthwith attains
Wisdom without their leave? and wherein lies
The offense, that Man should thus attain to know?
What can your knowledge hurt him, or this tree
Impart against his will, if all be his?
Or is it envy? and can envy dwell
In heavenly breasts? These, these, and many more
Causes import your need of this fair fruit.
Goddess humane, reach then, and freely taste!

(From Paradise Lost *by John Milton)*

Timeline of the Modern Era: 1440 - 1914

1440: Johannes Gutenberg invents the printing press.

1453: Byzantium falls to the Ottoman Turks; Eastern intellectuals move West.

1521-1618: The Reformation

1521: Luther defends his works at the Diet of Worms; the Reformation begins.

1543-1689: The Scientific Revolution

1555: Charles V agrees to the Peace of Augsburg; "Cuius regio, eius religio," the religion of the ruler becomes the religion of the ruled.

1618-1689: The baroque era

1618-1648: The Thirty Years' War, which begins religious and ends political: Christendom is shattered.

1649: The Regicide

1689-1789: The Enlightenment

1689: Sir Isaac Newton publishes Principia Mathematica; the clock becomes the organizing principle of society.

1789-1815: The French Revolution

1756-1763: The Seven Years' War; European wars become global events.

1789: The French Revolution, in which French republicans embrace Rousseau's philosophy and the American precedent

1799: Napoleon Bonaparte takes control of the Revolution as Enlightened despot and Romantic hero.

1815-1871: The age of national unifications

1815: Napoleon is defeated; Europe seeks balance.

1848: A wave of democratic revolutions are suppressed in Europe.

1914: The First World War shatters the Enlightenment myth of perpetual progress; the post-modern world is born.

The Rules of Decorum

Many private schools include an honor code in their student handbook, although I have found most honor codes simply too generic to actually govern student behavior in the classroom. Honor codes are apt to condemn cheating and "disrespecting others," although most honor codes are little more than harmless works of bureaucracy which can be forgotten entirely after the first week of school. I am yet to find an honor code which inspires students or quickens the heart. Nonetheless, several years into my career, I was sufficiently tired of explaining (and adjudicating) the same issues of bad behavior over and over again that I decided to author my own honor code. Since adopting the use of a catechism, I have students copy out "the Decorum" (so I call it) by hand every year when they transcribe the catechism into their test books. The Decorum is as follows:

1. If you are tired when you come to class, there is no need for you to announce this to your peers. If you have stayed up late studying, do not boast of how hard you have worked. Do not demand sympathy from others, or from your teachers, just because you are tired. Your friends are tired, too, as are your teachers, many of whom have children to care for. Loudly announcing that you are tired as you come into class is often a way of suggesting to the teacher, "Don't bother me today," and a way of suggesting to your peers, "You will have to carry the conversation today." As Christ instructs those who fast, if you are tired when it is time for class, splash a little water on your face and put on a cheerful expression "so that it will not be obvious to others that you are

fasting (from sleep), but only to your Father, who is unseen; and your Father, who sees what is done in secret, will reward you."

2. A school is a place for learning. A book is a thing for learning. A student is a person for learning. Additionally, there are attitudes for learning and postures for learning. While in class, sit up straight and keep your feet on the floor. Do not put your head on the table or prop your feet up on the chairs. Treat your body as the outward, physical manifestation of your soul. If you conduct your body with dignity and respect, your soul will likely follow soon enough.

3. If you cannot remember what you read for homework just two nights ago, you have not done your homework. You should be able to answer simple questions about what you've read. If you are asked about an assigned text, the reply "I read it really late last night and I don't remember it" is not an acceptable excuse. It is an indication you have not done your work. Read slowly and patiently so that you are able to discuss assigned reading in class whenever the time comes.

4. The humanities are not graded the way math and science are graded. For example, if you take a math examination composed of ten problems and you answer seven correctly, you would expect a 70 percent. However, if you are assigned a thousand-word essay and only write seven hundred words, you should not expect a 70 percent. You have failed to complete the minimum requirements and may receive a 0 percent grade; you may

or may not be invited to resubmit the paper. Think of it like this, though. If you went to a restaurant and ordered a 10 oz steak which cost $10, and then received a 2 oz steak, you would send it back. You would not pay $2, eat it and leave.

5. Likewise, if you write a thousand-word essay which is uniformly terrible (endlessly redundant information, not proofread, few citations, etc.), you may receive a 0 percent. If a thousand-word essay is assigned, not just any thousand-word essay which is submitted will warrant a passing grade. It is even possible for an essay which receives a 0 percent to have some merit. Think of like it like this, if you went to a restaurant and ordered a 10 oz medium rare steak and then received a raw 10 oz steak, you would send it back. In sending the raw steak back, you would not be indicating the meat had no value, but simply that it was unacceptable in its present condition.

6. If you are assigned reading for homework and do not do that reading, you need to inform your teacher of that fact before class begins. The same goes for homework. If I am collecting homework and you do not have any to turn in, tell me; if you do not tell me at the time I am collecting homework, I will not accept it later.

7. Speak of this school with respect. If you have a grievance with any decision made by a teacher, the staff, or the board, those grievances should be addressed privately to a teacher or to the principal, who will be glad to sit down with you and hear out your complaint.

Speaking critically of the school to your peers, especially on school grounds, is inappropriate and disrespectful. This means that all complaints about the dress code, assemblies, homework load, grades, teachers, and so forth must be directed to a teacher or the administration. Ours is a God who takes complaints seriously, but you must direct your complaints to someone who can do something about them. Your peers can do nothing about the dress code. The principal can, though.

8. Learning to be a good student in high school is preparation for being a good student in college and being a good employee when you are older. Having good manners is essential for being a good student. As such, you should not be seen yawning in class, or turning your head to look at the clock. If you must yawn, cover your mouth and do it discreetly. If you are fastidious about knowing what time it is, wear a watch and check it covertly. Yawning and looking at the clock are signs of boredom, even if you are not bored. While I will be understanding if I see you yawn or check the clock, your employers and college profs might not be.

9. If you talk in class, you must contribute to a group conversation. Private conversations with people beside you and across the table are not polite. "Private conversations" are not limited to spoken words. Silently mouthed conversations and hand gestures back and forth are just as distracting to your classmates as spoken conversations.

10. I host an after-school detention on Mondays. It runs

from 3:10 until 4:00. A scheduled sports practice is not a viable excuse for not coming to detention. If you are given detention, we will listen to a Johnny Cash record together and talk about how to become better people.

11. If you believe a grade you have received is unfair, please come and speak with me after class. Present your case. I am a reasonable person, but from time to time I will misunderstand your essays. When this happens, come and explain yourself and I will reconsider your grade. When you present your case, your case should stand on the merits of your own work; do not compare your work with the work of a classmate who scored better and allege your work and your classmate's work are essentially identical.

12. When you struggle with the material, talk with me. Do not wait until the end of the trimester (when report cards are about to come out and you are unhappy with your grade) and say, "Well, I've had a very hard time understanding this class." You are obligated to bring such concerns to me as they occur, not merely when you are getting nervous about your grade.

13. Do not begin packing up your things until you have been dismissed. There should be no rustling of papers and backpacks in the final moments of class while a lecture is going on, or reading is going on, or discussion is going on. Students who begin getting ready to go before class is over will stay after class for five minutes.

14. If you are not present for a test or quiz, you will re-

ceive a 0 for that test or quiz until you make it up. It is not the teacher's responsibility to track you down to take a test or quiz. Rather, it is your responsibility to track the teacher down and arrange a time you can take the test or quiz you missed. You will need to be vigilant in tracking the teacher down to take tests or quizzes.

15. Enter class silently. Once you are in the classroom, class has begun. Silence helps prepare the mind to yield, to receive, to concentrate.

16. Respect must be shown to the task and work of education. Conduct yourself with dignity and speak of learning as a worthy goal. Do not disrespect the work of education by parading your disinterest in learning before your peers. If you waste your entire weekend playing video games, do not make light of this on Monday morning. Do not make light of God by speaking of shameful, vicious, and slothful things as though they are enviable and good.

17. Do not ask, "How can I get a better grade in your class?" The answer to this question will always be, "Do better." Ask instead, "How can I do better in your class?" In like fashion, do not say, "I am worried about my grade in your class." Say instead, "I am worried that I am not learning enough in this class."

18. You may not doodle or draw pictures during class, and if you come to class having drawn all over your skin, especially your hands, you will be asked to go wash it off before you may come to class.

19. Use the restroom before you come to class. No one will be excused to the restroom in the last fifteen minutes of class. If you ask to use the restroom during class, you may go, but you will be required to stay after class for five minutes.

20. If you are falling asleep in class, you will be sent to the office. Please do not think I am cross with you if you are sent to the office. We all fall asleep sometimes, including myself, and it is no sin. However, if you are falling asleep in class, there is no point in you remaining in class, and you will be a distraction to others.

21. If you are asked to leave class for any reason, do not sigh and huff and perform your displeasure. If you do this, you will only make the situation worse for yourself. Conduct yourself with dignity. Collect your things and depart from class like a gentleman or a lady.

22. Rubrics are not used for the grading of tests, quizzes, or essays. In the humanities, grades are subjective, but not arbitrary, and objective reasons can be given to explain any grade. If you would like further explanation of a grade you have received or a comment you receive in the margins, you will need to schedule a meeting with myself, and I will be happy to explain everything in much greater detail.

23. Students who rarely participate in class will likely not learn much, not enjoy class, and not score well. Students who ask questions, converse, discuss, opine, appear engaged, and respond to their classmates will do well. Fur-

ther, students who contribute nothing to class should expect frank, curt assessments when parent-teacher conferences roll around. I will simply tell your mother and father, "Your child contributes nothing to class. I do not have anything more to tell you."

24. If an assignment comes due and is collected in class, but you have not finished the assignment, you must inform me of this fact when the assignment is collected. Do not simply *not turn in the assignment* and say nothing about it. Failing to inform me at the time may mean the work is not acceptable later.

25. Most grades will fall into one of the following five categories.

A zero. This work does not meet minimum standards for submission. While this work is not devoid of value, there is not much evidence that the student understood the assignment and made an honest, valiant effort to meet the requirements of the assignment.

A 74 percent. An honest effort was made to meet the requirements of the assignment and the student enjoyed some success in this effort. The work is a partial success and exhibits some knowledge. However, there were significant aspects of the work which were deficient, lacking. Comment has been made on how this work can be improved. The student should note criticism and recall it when he sets to work next, striving to improve in the ways he was deficient.

An 84 percent. Good, not great. Good enough. The student's work is passable and exhibits an acceptable knowledge and opinion of the subject. The student's work is not lacking in any necessary way, but neither is there a brilliance to the work which warrants praise. The work does not require modification. The work covered a predictable range of information and opinion, and the opinions were expressed reasonably enough. The work is neither excellent nor terrible, thus it does not warrant comment from the teacher. If this work were the food at a restaurant, the patron would neither complain about the food, but neither would he be eager to return.

A 94 percent. Great work. This work is better than average, exceptional, worth commenting on, and excellence is evident in the clarity of thought and profundity of opinion. This is work of some degree of academic maturity and ambition. The student struggled and succeeded in making his thoughts memorable and compelling.

A 100 percent. A rarity which might only be glanced a few times over the course of the school year. Work which warrants such a score is worthy of the world of adults and might be mistaken for adult thought in another context.

I read the Decorum several times over the course of the year. It is especially valuable to review one month into the school year, as well as when students return from Christmas break and spring break. I appeal to the Decorum often throughout the year, and I have attempted to word the thing in a sufficiently colorful manner so that it is not a drag to revisit every now and again.

CHAPTER FOUR

How to Write Your Own Catechism

Step One: Foundational Questions

The teacher who wants to write a catechism for his own class should begin with a series of foundational questions and answers which help students recall the purpose of education. These questions do not directly reference the content of the class, but frame everything which follows. Each of my catechisms begins with the same seven questions, all of which affirm the students as kings and queens who are responsible for attaining virtue and capable of doing so through their adoption into the suffering and glory of Jesus Christ. To be frank, the foundational questions should contain several long passages of Scripture which pertain to the pursuit of virtue because classical Christian education is not yet at such a place that teachers can insist on the necessity of good works without expecting pushback. Virtue and good works are often not regarded as a matter of life and death but as a super-fluous hobby of the pious. Nevertheless, students are not alone in needing daily reminders to do good. I have shared classrooms with teachers who wasted the first twenty minutes of every class period with pointless stories and banal jokes. I, too, feel the daily sting of St. James' charge that "faith without works is dead."

In the first several years that a catechism is employed, some adjustment and modification should be expected. If your cate-chism does not change at all between the first and second years you employ it, you are probably doing it wrong. Nonetheless, teachers should put more care into the foundational questions than any other part of the catechism; the stability of the foun-dational questions is paramount. The foundational questions should undergo the least modification from year to year. On days in which teachers must abbreviate the catechism (which should be done rarely), they will tend to recite the first several questions only. What is more, the foundational questions ought to be shared between all catechisms and all grades, and perhaps even different departments of the school. Thus, a greater num-ber of students are committing time to these questions. While I am confident my students will remember *most* of the catechism for many years to come, a teacher ought to wager the founda-tional questions will be present in students' minds for the rest of their lives.

QUESTIONS ARE MORE THAN CUES

Not all of the questions and answers in the catechism sync up perfectly, and this is by design. For instance, I ask my students, "What does it mean to be human?" and they respond, "The vir-tues are faith, hope, love, wisdom, justice, courage, and temper-ance." The unsubtly hidden assumption between the question and the answer is that being human means being virtuous. In prior years, I asked, "What are the virtues?" and students responded by listing off all seven, but I have gradually realized that I get more usage out of the question if there is a greater distance to the answer. Elsewhere in the catechism, students ask, "What is temptation and what is virtue?" and they respond with a long passage from *Jane Eyre* wherein Jane describes why she will not stay with Rochester. The question which sets off the long citation from Bronte might have just as easily been "What is conservatism?" or "How is virtue its own reward?" Jane's speech is a forthright acknowledgement that her stomach is telling her to disobey her heart and mind; overpowering her stomach is unpleasant, but she must remain faithful to the "laws and principles" she was taught as a child, for those laws and principles were given to her in anticipation of the awful situation in which she finds herself in chapter twenty-seven. If phrased properly, a catechism question can be much more than a cue for the answer.

Let us say a teacher wants to include the Beatitudes in his catechism. Let us also suppose that the first question on his catechism is "Gentlemen, what are you?" and the answer is "I am a king for I rule myself." As opposed to following the first question up with "What are the Beatitudes?" and having the students recite the opening verses of the Sermon on the Mount, he might ask, "How should we then live?" The latter question reinforces the weight of the Beatitudes, as opposed to the morally neutral phrasing of the first question. Virtually every question in the catechism can be worded with such force. Do not ask, "What are the vices?" Instead, ask, "What are the works of the Devil?" Do not ask, "What are the words of the Nicene Creed?" Ask, "What is the Christian faith?"

Step Two: Curriculum, Condensed

The bulk of the catechism should come from classic texts which are read in class. The catechism is a condensed curriculum. Questions and answers included, a catechism which takes seven to eight minutes to say will be around thirteen hundred words long. Imagine, for a moment, dearest literature teacher, that as opposed to teaching eight books next year—perhaps three thousand pages, or nearly a million words—you have merely thirteen hundred words. *Frankenstein* is gone. Burke is gone. Rousseau is gone. Dickens is gone. Your whole modern European curriculum is gone. Or, rather, everything you want from Burke and Rousseau and Dickens must be refined down to just two and a half pages. The purpose of the catechism is not to give every classic author their fair share of space. Canonized villains like Rousseau and Marx do not deserve equal time in the catechism with canonized heroes like Homer and Burke.

The catechism should convey a strong moral vision, not merely a summary of content. It is a *catechism*, after all, and not a survey. If the catechism would prove inoffensive to men who embrace falsehood and preach deception, then the catechism is worthless. If a secularist college professor actively advancing zeitgeisty politics would read the catechism and say, "Well, this is a fair synopsis of modern content," then the catechism has no real value. The catechism is a preparation for life, a preparation for the Judgment, not a preparation for the SAT. Judiciously using space in the catechism will mean teachers grant priority to the truth, not to a diversity of opinions. That said, teachers should strive to write catechisms which reference every book in the curriculum. If there are seven books in the sophomore literature program, each book should contribute at least one question to the catechism. Let us say that one of those books is *The Communist Manifesto* and another is *The Abolition of Man*. It should be sufficient to quote forty or fifty words from Marx, but two hundred from Lewis.

Quotations from auxiliary texts, secondary sources, or commentaries should be used sparingly in the catechism because they do not carry the moral or mystical weight which attends traditional texts. A teacher cannot "vouch" for contemporary commentaries, even very good ones, because the most venerable endorsement which can be supplied to any text is the endorsement of time, and a classical teacher should not want his students to think that "very good modern books" have the same value as "very good old books." Who can say how many theology programs (at venerable universities) have quickly gone off the rails because, after twenty generations of teaching Augustine's *The City of God*, some plucky upstart thought it permissible to exchange the most well-respected theology text in existence for "something quite good which was written last year by this guy from Michigan I like." Within just a few years of the teacher's departure, the curriculum becomes a free-for-all.

The teacher who assembles a catechism should do so assuming that someone else will take over the class in ten years, and that the new teacher will use all the materials left behind as a guide. What kind of guide will the catechism be? The teacher who leaves behind a catechism with two citations from contemporary sources should assume his successor will feel at liberty to compile a catechism with three or four contemporary citations. The teacher who leaves behind a catechism with no contemporary sources should assume his successor will feel comfortable doubling that number. Needless to say, the teacher whose catechism is entirely bereft of anything non-canonical is far more likely to establish something immovable, stable, and timeless. As soon as any exception has been made for modern preferences, a significant breach will become thinkable.

Step Three: Presentation

If significant care is put into compiling the catechism, great care must also be taken in the way the catechism is presented to students. On the day the catechism is first handed out, teachers should be wholly transparent with students. If the catechism has been prefaced by years of failure to communicate content in a memorable way, teachers should own up to this fact. "How many of you still remember the Stuart line, which I tested you on last year in April?" When the class laughs this question off, the teacher should laugh it off, as well. If there is one lesson which all Christians can learn from Martin Luther—be they Catholic, Orthodox, Presbyterian, or Lutheran—it is that reform is both embarrassing and expensive. A great many of the reforms which Luther ultimately prompted in Catholic Christianity were reforms Catholics themselves had sought out for quite some time, and yet lacked a reason to pursue full bore. Luther pressed these issues with no regard to cost, though, and the reforms which had formerly been attempted on the cheap then had to be pursued at great expense. The teacher moving from a system of assessment wherein students cram, pass, and forget the material must tacitly admit to wasting students' time if he wants to institute a catechism. The temptation to run reform on the cheap, by which I mean *not* admitting guilt nor complicit involvement in superfluous and risible systems, is nearly overwhelming, for the teacher will think that such an admission of guilt will sink the respect which students formerly had for the teacher or the academy. However, real reform requires humility.

When the catechism is first handed out, teachers should conduct polls among students about what content from previous years is still available to the memory. While much content which was "memorized" in previous years is now gone, what content which was "memorized" is yet present for recall? A great deal of the content which is still present for students will be content memorized as a class, in ceremony. Most of what has been forgotten will have been memorized individually, through uncertain and unpredictable means. Teachers would do well to recognize that much of the frustration which students feel toward school grows out of the sense that their time is being wasted in useless, arbitrary requirements, and every teacher knows the frustration which attends hearing the administration is adding another arbitrary requirement (test prep cards, lesson plan abstracts, final exam proposal sheets) onto their already full workload. "What use will this serve? Who could possibly think this will be of value to us or the school?" Students ask the same questions every time they are asked to memorize the Stuart line or the ancient Assyrian kings, for they know full well—before the "memorization" has even begun—that everything will be forgotten within two weeks. Even good teachers are complicit in such systems of time-wasting and hoop-jumping.

The institution of the catechism ought to come as a relief to everyone, then, and the teacher should express this relief when moving students from a system which wastes everyone's time to a system wherein canonized texts are memorized for life. If some kind of joy, liberty, and emancipation does not accompany the institution of the catechism, the teacher does not know what the catechism really is.

CHAPTER FIVE

An Anthology of Tests

I would like to offer readers a host of different tests which I have given, as well as some direction on the point of the test and how the test grew out of my time teaching the book. While anyone is free to give such tests whether or not they use a catechism, these tests fulfill the promises inherent in the daily recitation of canonical texts. The respect paid to the masters in the catechism allows the catechized to speak, but only within limits set by the masters. The sheer objectivity of the catechism is balanced with the subjectivity of tests, and so every class is both physical and spiritual, fact and opinion, tangible and unapproachable.

One of the greatest benefits of a daily catechism is that teachers are free to give far more interesting, far more humane tests.

It is reasonable to expect that every high school class would require students to memorize a great deal of material; however, as has already been shown, information which students "memorize" for a closed-book test is quickly forgotten. Having put all the objective information he wants memorized into the catechism, the teacher may allow students to use their books and notes while taking exams. The teacher can send nearly all tests and quizzes home with students. In the first several years I taught, before I instituted a catechism, I lost nearly 15 percent of my class time to testing and quizzing. Each year, I spent well north of thirty hours in the classroom silently watching my students write essays and fill in blanks.

If readers have balked at the idea of spending seven minutes a day reciting a catechism, remember that the catechism means silently proctoring exams largely becomes a thing of the past. The catechism means open books, open notes, and such assessments can be taken at home. In the last five years, I have written more than four hundred articles for the CiRCE Institute and more than one hundred reviews for FilmFisher, and all of these essays were written open book, open note. I cannot imagine being asked to write an essay about *Paradise Lost* after having read the book once, and not being allowed access to the book to remind myself of, say, exact dialogue in particular passages. I do not see the point in asking questions on exams like, "What was the name of the demon in *Paradise Lost* who built Pandemonium?" Why this fact is worth knowing off the top of your head is anyone's guess. The teacher knows the name of the demon who built Pandemonium simply because he looked it up before writing the question, or because he has read *Paradise Lost* five times. Any effort the student puts into "memorizing" the name of this or that demon is time taken away from genuine contemplation and enjoyment of the book. One does not need to read *Paradise Lost* to know this demon's name. The teacher should take care to ask questions which cannot be looked up. If the teacher assigns reading homework, a daily reading quiz can be given which is three or four questions long and takes a mere thirty seconds to fill out. Accountability is good and helpful (to a degree), but accountability is not really *educational*. So far as the classroom is concerned, accountability is a *start*, but "The name of the demon who . . ." is an accountability question, which means it has no place on the final.

I recall, many years ago, sitting down to grade a stack of papers one evening and finding myself quite literally in tears after half an hour because I was so bored with what I was reading and I had more than forty essays left to read. This was hardly the first time I had cried real tears in frustration with the banality of student writing; however, on this particular evening, it struck me that I was entirely to blame for my own suffering. It was I, in fact, who had written a very dull essay prompt, and it was only fair that the essays returned to me were also dull. The test prompt in question had been written with embarrassing haste. It was probably something like, "Some people claim that Satan is the real hero of *Paradise Lost*. Argue against this claim and use three separate citations from the book to prove your thesis." I may have required as many as one thousand words to satisfy this flaccid, lifeless query. Such questions are scarcely better than asking for the name of the demon who built Pandemonium. While I did not want students to merely supply names or dates, I was basically asking them to recapitulate several lectures I had already given in class. While I offered everyone the use of their books, I was asking them to take a cursory glance in the margins and find the passages wherein we had discussed the question of Satan being the hero. The prompt was meant to reward students who had taken copious notes and to chastise those who hadn't, even though there is nothing necessarily virtuous about taking many notes. Even a very wicked person could have completed the assessment without ever needing to second-guess his own boredom with virtue. If a very wicked person could do very well on a theology exam or a philosophy quiz, the person who wrote the quiz is not likely teaching *virtue*, but facts. Facts have no moral weight.

Final Assessment on Paradise Lost

The first example is a final exam on *Paradise Lost* I gave after having not taught the book in three years. While I recalled enjoying the book, a fresh read proved the book was more concerned with education than I had previously recognized. Many chapters of the book are devoted to Adam's education in cosmology, philosophy, history, and so forth, and the purpose of Adam's education was wholly centered on man having all the tools he needed to fight temptation. As I taught the book, I figured it out, or else I figured out what had been (on earlier reads) a buried theme, hidden in plain sight. I suspect that many teachers have had similar experiences and know the thrill of chasing down some lately discovered theme. Some great lectures surprise even the teacher, who had planned on speaking of something conventional, yet finds the scent of some truffle hidden between the lines of the text and goes racing off like a bloodhound for treasure while the students huff to keep up. Typically, the emergence of some fresh discovery is likewise invigorating for the class, not just the teacher, but on this occasion, the class was hexed by some unaccountable boredom during the two or three days in which we discussed *Paradise Lost* as a treatise on education.

In the epic poem, Milton gives Adam two teachers, the archangels Raphael and Michael. Before the Fall, Raphael tutors Adam in a variety of liberal arts, though Adam is far more interested in talking of Eve and even goes so far as to ask Raphael if angels copulate. Raphael is austere, very proper, a teacher who refuses to pity the immaturity of his student, and after being asked about angelic copulation, he invents an excuse for the lesson to be over and promptly departs. In the end, a disordered affection for Eve proves Adam's downfall, and the attentive reader cannot help wondering how the story would have turned out differently if Raphael had not been so embarrassed to discourse on chastity with the same verve and thoroughness with which he lectured on history. After the Fall, God sends Michael to teach Adam and Eve about the future of evil on Earth. Michael is much less proper, much less reserved than Raphael, and Adam and Eve are appropriately rapt. Harrowing and fearsome, Michael's lectures sink deeply into Adam's psyche, whereas Raphael's dully bounce off.

Accordingly, I wrote the following exam:

Ten years from now, to your great surprise and mine, you become a teacher at a classical school.

You were marginally interested in great books while in high school, but then you went to college, and after a couple semesters living la bohème (couches, unnecessary road trips, skipping classes), you realized you were getting nowhere and actually began missing your old high school teachers. They seemed to care about virtue, and regardless of all those absurd homework assignments and their nit-picky insistence that you obey the dress code and not look at your cell phone in the men's room, what they really wanted was for you to be content with your life.

While in college, you realize your teachers were human, that they made mistakes, suffered, and wanted to keep you from needless suffering, despair, depression, vice, regret, and so forth. You switch your major from communications to classics, go to bed early, get up early, lose ten pounds, revisit Virgil, start singing in church again. You see the people around you collecting DUIs and Ws on their transcripts, as well as staggering debt from student loan money they are blowing on overpriced headphones, buffalo wings, jeans, and cologne. "Whatever. These are the best days of our lives," they say, but they tend to spend a lot of time on WebMD every Monday morning looking nervous. Looking back on your life, you see that you might have easily turned out the way they are turning out, that you might have squandered a chance at having a decent marriage, a healthy liver, and children who love you unconditionally. There but for the grace of God go I, you say. Just a little more vice and little less care for my soul and I might not have had the energy to turn back. I was never very bad. I was only a little bad, however . . . I could have easily decided to be very bad. You don't have children yet, but you are definitely marriage material. So many people around you are not, though.

After you graduate, you return to your old school to look around. All the same administrators and teachers and principals still work here, even years from now. You get a visitor's pass. You graduated from a decent college with a degree in classics. You even got a paper about the Iliad published in some journal somewhere. You owe the federal government thirty thousand dollars. You might have gotten away with owing less, but those first few semesters didn't get you many credits. You submit an application to teach at your old high school. If someone had told you years ago that you'd be back at this school, looking for a job, and really hoping that you'd get it, you would have laughed. Teachers might have laughed at that, too. They are quite surprised, but when you have your interview, you tell them about the course of your life. They even invite you to teach a class as part of the interview process. They observe your lesson, and you end up doing a chapter from Paradise Lost. You are excited and all the students give you the time of day because you are younger than their usual teacher, and the fact you have stylish clothes makes you something of a novelty.

You are hired. You are happy. You get an apartment, trade out your 1989 Civic and get a respectable looking car. You have a job teaching literature. You like literature. Everything looks very different from behind the lectern, though.

You are baffled when your students try to get away with things like passing notes, sending texts in the bathroom, talking during class, lying, turning in crumpled homework, lying to their parents about things you've said, not doing their homework, complaining about the dress code policy and fairness. You are not so much baffled with your students as you are baffled with yourself. These things upset you far more than you thought they would. Back when you were in high school, you said to yourself, "I don't know why teachers get so upset about this stuff. Teenagers are teenagers. It's not a big deal." You told yourself before starting this job as a teacher, "I'm going to be the cool teacher, but my students are also going to learn a lot, too!" Two weeks into your first year teaching senior literature, you find yourself getting flustered in class when students are not paying attention or becoming bored. You are staying up until one in the morning preparing lessons, but when you show up to class, no one looks at you when you speak. Often enough, you feel as though you are talking to no one but yourself. You sometimes lose your place in your notes and need a moment to collect yourself, and the students who don't really care about your class smirk at each other and make you feel like a fool. You also find that teachers have to be incredibly tight-lipped about everything. On one occasion you write, "Could do better" at the top of a test wherein a B student scored a low C. The following day an irate parent talks your ear off for forty-five minutes about how her son is "doing the best he can and really doesn't need your glib criticism," although you know this is absurd. Truth be told, you can recall a time when you were younger and you overheard your mother say the same thing to one of your teachers. Your mother said you were "doing the best you could." When she said this, you immediately felt guilty, for you knew it wasn't true. You tried hard every blue moon, but honestly . . . doing "the best you could"? Wow. Is anyone doing the best they can?

The first semester passes slowly. You share your concerns with other teachers, although they don't entirely take you seriously. The older, more experienced teachers simply nod when you describe your woes. "The first year is always the hardest," they say. You reply, "Why do you say that? Does everyone listen to your lectures with interest? Do they all keep quiet in your classes?" The older teachers just smile. You wonder what you have gotten yourself into. Around this time, you find out that one of your old classmates—someone who went to the school where you now teach—has just been arrested for committing a violent crime. You recommit your efforts to your work.

Finally, the time rolls around to teach Paradise Lost. *You found the book only a little moving in high school, but many of the conversations you had during your study of the book stayed with you, and you have sometimes said to friends, "Of all the books I read in high school,* Paradise Lost *is one that stayed with me the longest after I read it." While it might seem overdramatic to say so, you credit the fact you were able to turn your life around with a few particular lines and scenes in Milton's great poem.*

On the day that you get to book IX, wherein the Fall of Man occurs, you greatly look forward to class. Your students have been fairly bored of late, but you have prepared a lecture which you believe they will find genuinely intriguing. You are going to teach them

something profound, in a lucid and moving way, that they will re-
member for years to come. You are going to teach them to be good.
You are going to show them the importance of being virtuous, of
rightly ordering their loves.

Class begins, and within moments you realize that despite your
fascinating claims about free will and Milton's theology, no one is
listening to you.

Suddenly, you are cut to the heart. You are trying to help these
students become good, content, happy. You do not want them to be
arrested for a violent crime, but they do not care. You are trying to
save them from misery. You know the temptations ahead of them.
And for a moment, you are baffled once again. You are baffled at
the strangeness of the situation. One human being is trying to help
other human beings be happy, and the other human beings are not
really interested in hearing about how to be happy. They are bored.
You are nearly begging them to be good, and giving them good
reasons to be good, and they are falling asleep.

Given that you are trying to do them a service, why are they bored?
You scrap your lesson plan. You realize in a moment that your
approach to the whole thing was way too Raphael. What your stu-
dents need is Michael. What do you tell them about Adam's deci-
sion to sin? Use what you have learned from Michael's lesson to
Adam late in Paradise Lost *to offer up an exhortation to be good.*
How will your students be tempted? Why should they be good?
Why should they flee temptation?

In some sense, this test is merely "An eye for an eye, and a
tooth for a tooth . . ." Despite modern disdain for Moses, the *lex*
talionis aims toward the development of self-awareness. "An eye

for an eye" assumes that sin results from a failure of the imagination and that the criminal lacks the creative power to see the world from the perspective of his victim. The *lex talionis* forces the perspective of the victim upon the criminal, thus collapsing the ontological distance between the two. "An eye for an eye" does not inflict arbitrary or generic pain upon the criminal, but the particular pain of the victim.

With this particular test, I asked my students to take my place, and not merely my place as a teacher, but as a teacher who was desperate to teach virtue, and whose students were largely uninterested. From time to time, teachers ask students to give a ten-minute presentation on subjects germane to class, however, such presentations are not really concerned with giving students a sense of the plight of the teacher. Most students are willing to indulge their peers for a few minutes, because student lectures are an extreme novelty, and there is much to laugh about later, for the lectures are generally not very good and everyone knows this. While putting students in the position of the teacher is a worthy goal, in order to accomplish such a change of perspective, the student presentation would need to fill an entire hour. Unless a student presentation were allowed to run embarrassingly, uncomfortably long, the presenter would never really experience the difficulty of the teacher.

As opposed to beating around the bush, this *Paradise Lost* test spelled out the whole scenario in which I wanted my students to find themselves, complete with thinly-veiled characters and forthright descriptions of their boredom and ennui. If this seems like cheating, recall that Christ employs similar strategies when testing the affections of the religious leaders of his day (Matt. 21:33-41), as does Nathan the prophet when rebuking King David (2 Sam. 12:7).

When we began our study of *Paradise Lost*, there was no way I could have known the final assessment would turn out this way. The worst teacher I ever knew taught theology and literature and gave the same tests and quizzes year in and year out, no change. He once showed me a binder filled with all the same tests for all the same lessons from all the same great works of literature. In the several years we worked together, I do not remember the fellow ever asking me a question. We met early in my career; however, even at that time, the idea of giving the same tests over the same books year after year seemed like giving the same birthday card with the same handwritten note to my daughter every year. Nothing changed since last year, dad? This is not to say one should never give the same test twice, but it behooves a teacher of virtue to deal with the particular struggles of a class over a book. With some books, those struggles are perennial, but not with all. Every journey though Milton, Dante, or Homer will be different than the last time, for classics evolve between readings. A first read of *Paradise Lost* and a second read of *Paradise Lost* cannot be compared—they have no more in common than *Blade Runner* and *Leaves of Grass*. The teacher who always gives the same tests over Homer is either not paying attention to Homer, or he is paying attention, but lacks the profundity of spirit to be changed by Homer. Homer strikes at the deep end of a man, if he has a deep end, but some men wither in the sun for they "have no root," as Christ says.

Final Assessment on Early Modern Humanities

How do you write an exam which encompasses Milton, Burke, Rousseau, Shakespeare, Shelley and Bronte? You don't. But you must fail at the task as elegantly as possible. Multiple-choice exams are rightly chagrined in classical education, and yet this rule allows a few exceptions.

One of the great unsung heroes of the New Testament is the nameless centurion who happily proclaims himself a "man under authority," who answers to those above and commands those beneath. Classicists should maintain a healthy respect for old traditions, even the old traditions of other churches, and the standard answer to the sticky theological inquiries of a student ought to be, "That is a question for your pastor." Classical educators should end up funneling a massive amount of intellectual, theological, and pastoral work off to the priests and pastors of their students. As an Orthodox Christian in an ecumenical school, I can field a few questions from interested Presbyterian students on the matter of relics and icons, but I am hasty to remind students who become very curious about Orthodoxy that they are already spiritually accountable to people who have strong opinions on these matters. "Your pastor is the one to ask about icons," I say, "or your parents, perhaps."

Similarly, I am vexed when others trespass on my authority. My favorite meeting is the kind where someone is obviously in charge, calling the shots, and I am merely obediently making notes on what I must do. As an educator, obedience to properly sanctioned authorities is a great interest of mine: I do not want to raise rebels but students who will obey their elders, their pastors, and their priests. As such, I do not believe my students need to figure out what they believe, but to recognize the proper authorities to whom they owe allegiance, those who are materially and spiritually accountable for their well-being. Given the ongoing, perpetual, total disintegration of confidence in authority which typifies the modern era, the culmination of my Early Modern Humanities is often an assessment like this:

Reflect on the state of your own soul for a moment. Let us assume that you are not merely the product of your environment, but that there is something transcendent about your being, that while you might have been born in a different time and a different place, you would have nonetheless still been yourself. Under which of the following historical circumstances would your soul have stood the best likelihood of being very, very righteous?

a. I would have done best during the age of the martyrs. I believe I have the faith to survive the martyr's test. Given the sins to which I am tempted, I would have thrived in a situation of intense, violent, terrifying persecution.

b. I would have done best during the medieval era as a poor onion farmer; I would not have had access to a Bible, but I don't read the Bible much anyway. I would not have been aware of apostasy and infidelity to God, for everyone I would have known would have been a Christian; given how my life is likely to turn out, I wish that denying the faith really wasn't a possibility. I would be willing to trade all the freedom I have as a twenty-first-century American for a life of ignorance, hard work, and spiritual mediocrity.

c. I would have done best during the Renaissance era. I have the kind of faith that would not be shaken by witnessing the highest-ranking officials in the Church become avaricious dictators. I am fairly comfortable with having corrupt clergymen in my church. I am fairly corrupt, after all.

d. I would have done best during the early modern era. When faced with the complexity of decisions the common man had to make about theological matters, I doubt I would have been intimidated into disinterest in religion. I am also the kind of person who has the faith and stamina (and cares enough about theology) to pack up my belongings and move to a new part of the world, probably *to become considerably poorer, simply because I refused to accept a doctrine about the Lord's Supper which I didn't believe, and which the local magistrate was coercing people into accepting.*

e. I would have done best in the early American West, where there were no churches. I don't need to go to church to remain faithful to God. My love of God can sustain itself without the support of anyone else.

f. I would do best in contemporary America. Despite the endless temptations and distractions from the things of God, I still devote several hours every day (even during the summer) to reading my Bible and performing works of charity and mercy. I rarely spend time on amusement and entertainment; I primarily use the great freedom afforded to moderns for cultivating a virtuous soul.

Explain your answer.

These options are, of course, not entirely fair, and some of the most attractive options require tacit admissions of spiritual sloth. However, the unfairness of the options makes them realistic, for very few people attend a church which entirely suits their tastes, and the Devil is fond of reminding us of all the exceptions we take to our churches. The more tenaciously the Devil can align us with our exceptions, and even reduce us to our exceptions, the more we will believe our churches are lucky to have us. A certain kind of multiple choice exam can pull students back from their exceptions, though. When asked open-endedly, "What do you think of free will?" is not a reasonable test question, for it overvalues student opinions and puts undue pressure on the student to reinvent the wheel. A classically minded student, regardless of his denomination, should respond to such a question with a summary of what his church teaches on the matter. On the other hand, a teacher might ask, "What do you think of free will?" and then offer a series of options, each of which represented the various traditional or denominational accounts of human freedom and divine power. Christians may criticize the zeitgeist for inventing (from whole cloth) new definitions of gender, marriage, and personhood, however, so long as we allow ninth-grade boys to lead Bible studies and encourage students to make up answers to theological questions as they go along, we are no better. Novel definitions of gender are far less serious than novel interpretations of St. Paul's epistle to the Romans. A certain kind of multiple-choice question can corral theological and philosophical possibilities in a powerful way. As for the multiple-choice test offered here, I even invited students to describe, in the explanation of their answer, why the options were unfair, if they were so inclined.

The wise teacher must strike a balance between the profound distinctiveness and uniqueness of every individual student, and the manner in which classicism and Christianity call individuals into established, dogmatic patterns of thought and living. Students need to understand that they are not free to think and say whatever they like, for that is bondage to the self and captivity to what is passing and fashionable. When the batholithic preoccupations of the Western tradition are on the line—questions about sin and law and grace and war and justice and mercy—a classical student should be comfortable with the fact that he may not invent a valid and venerable thought on the spot. Classicism presumes that the student who invents a wholly original theory of the atonement should at least be smirked at, not praised for his inventiveness. If theology and philosophy teachers opened the year with, "In this class, we're not going to spend time discussing theories or opinions which are less than fifty years old," they would likely save themselves weeks every year which could be devoted to Augustine or Plato or Pascal. And this, not because every theory or opinion of the last fifty years is invalid, but because the theories and opinions of the last fifty years are primarily what life outside of academia is devoted to. If school is going to be a safe place for anybody and anything, it ought to be a safe place for those long gone, because in our bridge-burning Enlightened age, few people have it harder than the dead.

Final Assessment on the Divine Comedy

When I begin teaching Dante, I tell my students that the *Comedy* touches on every moral and ethical matter about which they might have questions. "What do you want the *Comedy* to teach you?" I ask, because the *Comedy* is about just about everything. Any assessment on the *Divine Comedy* given in high school is simply a placeholder assessment in lieu of the real assessment. The real assessment occurs fifteen years after graduation, when the student is a husband, a father, and realizes he has developed an infatuation with a woman he works with. There are no grades given on this assessment, or else the grade is measured in children's tears.

The placeholder assessment should have something in common with the real assessment, though. To this end, my final exam on the *Comedy* presupposes the student has lately discovered one of their peers in the midst of an existential crisis and must offer counsel. What follows is the last test I gave during freshman year:

> *Part One: The Problem. Imagine, for a moment, that you have a friend at this school whom you have known since second grade. Let us call him Mark. In elementary school, you played together.*

Then you learned to ride bicycles together. Then you were in boy scouts together. However, during sophomore year, Mark has begun to struggle, while you have not.

High school sophomores are closer to college applications than they are to middle school, and something clicks in the back of your head during the summer between freshman year and sophomore year which clues you in to this sobering fact. Quite a lot changes in the summer before sophomore year. It is this summer in which many students get their first real jobs, the kind of jobs where taxes are taken out of every paycheck. Getting a job and having a little more money in your pocket changes you. You begin depending on your parents less, asking your parents for less, going out more, and dressing yourself in a manner more to your taste. There are a great many things about which your parents have said, "When you get a job, you can do that," and now you have a job.

Let us say that when you come back to school next year, sophomore year, Mark is really still stuck in freshman year. Nothing happened for him over the summer. Nothing clicked for him. He didn't get a job. He has not yet figured out that he is closer to adulthood than childhood, and he has not caught a vision of why adulthood is preferable. He begins the year still behaving as though all the same jokes and gags which had purchasing power in eighth grade are still viable currency. He is incapable of taking anything seriously at all. He makes a laugh of everything. He could have gotten a job over the summer, but his parents did not make him do so, and thus he wasted his time playing Halo all day. He has not purchased himself clothes that he likes, is uninterested in the clothes he is given to wear, and so he does not take much care to look presentable. When he told jokes back in eighth grade which disgusted the girls, he got respect from the other boys, including you. But now Mark is like kryptonite to girls, and girls scatter when he appears, which means none of the guys want anything to do with him anymore either. He still looks for high fives when he fails a test, but no one appreciates his rebel soul any longer.

The problem is not merely one of appearances, for Mark is still telling dead baby jokes, harassing girls, and mocking the Indian janitor's accent. While you are still young, you have seen human beings fail to become adults. You have an uncle who is forty-one, but who never really became an adult. He is an embarrassment to the family. Being an adult is like being a policeman. You can try to become a policeman and fail, and you can similarly fail to become an adult. Nothing changes for Mark over the course of the school year, and by the time May rolls around, you have begun to wonder how failed adults get started on the road to failure. "Probably," you suppose, "by living like my idiot friend Mark." What you really want to do is take Mark aside and say, "What's wrong with you?" But who are you to talk that way? You're only fifteen. What do you know? Besides, sometimes you still laugh at his jokes.

But then one day, a week before the school year ends, Mark asks if the two of you can sit together at lunch, and the ridiculous grin and funny voice he always uses are gone, and he sounds like a real person—maybe even a wounded person. At lunch, Mark talks straight with you. He opens the conversation by soberly saying, "Look, this year hasn't been great for me. No one likes me anymore. No one even wants to sit near me. No one ever texts me back. Only two people came with me to the movies on my birthday and I invited twenty people." Because the truth is often shameful, you begin to worry that maybe you should tell Mark a few lies so that the situation will feel less awkward. But you don't. Mark keeps talking, "And I get it. Something is wrong with me. I feel stupid. Not stupid, but

*like a little kid. I feel like I'm still stuck in eighth grade. Like grow-
ing up isn't happening to me. I want to grow up, I want to . . . have
opinions about colleges and all that. But . . . Look, do you think
I'm shallow?"* And as opposed to lying to Mark, or downplaying his
concern, you say, "Yes, Mark, I do think you're shallow."
Mark is not angry. He is relieved that someone has spoken the
truth to him, because when people speak the truth, there is necessarily hope, as well. Mark asks, "How do you become not shallow?"

Part Two: What You Know. In the beginning, Dante knows he
should leave the dark wood and ascend the backlit mountain to be
with God, but he does not want to do so. Halfway up the mountain,
he is beset by three temptations, and because Dante is shallow, he
retreats. He is unwilling to overcome his sin. He is shallow in that
he knows what is best but does not care. Dante has heard the Gospel. He has been baptized. However, like the seed which falls on
shallow soil and springs up quickly but withers in the sun because
it has no root, Dante responds quickly to the light of God, which he
sees beyond the mountain, but the Gospel in his soul withers under
the pressure of temptation. His soul is shallow. His soul has become
shallow by caring too much for trivial things and too little for deep
things. As he does not love deep things, neither is he deep.

At the conclusion of the Comedy, the vision ends and Dante must
find himself again on the mountain above the dark woods, halfway
to the top, once more beset by temptation. And yet we are confident
that his soul has deepened. During his education through Hell,
Earth, and Heaven, Dante's soul became the "good ground" Christ
speaks of in the parable of the sower, and the Word now has room
to grow, to lay down heavy roots, and to produce an abundance
of fruit. The education offered by Virgil and Beatrice is a classical
education, a liberal arts education, which cannot save Dante, for

Dante is not being forced to go to the Empyrean in chains. Rather, canto by canto, Dante is given room to contemplate and meditate on God, and his spirit deepens (like a coastal shelf) and grows more and more free.

Part Three: What You Do. *Using all that you have gleaned from Dante in our time studying the* Comedy, *advise your friend Mark on how to not be a shallow person. This essay should be a thousand words long and written in the first person.*

This is not the kind of test which is quickly glossed. After reading this prompt, I fielded questions for more than ten minutes. The questions came in slowly, for all the freshman had immediately begun comparing themselves with Mark and wondering, "Am I like that? Which of my friends is the most like Mark?" In the same way that the mere mention of "good posture" causes most students to subtly sit up straight, so the question of shallowness induced immediate, acute self-assessment. As opposed to blandly asking students what more is required of a sophomore than a freshman, I assumed they knew greater burdens of emotional and social responsibility were being added to their souls as they grew older. While they found this alarming, neither were they entirely surprised. Most people are simply surprised at how early old age comes.

For most of my students, completing the assignment meant speaking as though they had attained a level of maturity that they had not yet attained—but which they knew was necessary in order to enter the world of adulthood. The assignment does not call for a synopsis of Dante, but for students to approach moral struggle from Dante's position. Students who wrote mediocre essays were given to saying, at some point, "Mark, do you remember reading the *Divine Comedy*?" followed by a recapitulation of the plot and a few homiletic lessons derived from a basic outline of the story. The best essays, however, rarely or never made direct reference to the *Comedy*, but addressed Mark's shallowness with a discussion of the major themes of the poem: knowledge, desire, the will, and rightly ordered loves. Such advice was not really about Dante, but from Dante, or the student's best imitation of him. Some of the best student work I have ever received is prompted by a request that students pretend to be wiser and more lucid than they are. Every act of imitation is an act of becoming. Inasmuch as an imitation is sound, it is no mere imitation, but transformation.

Final Assessment on Medieval Humanities

As often as the teacher can make it so, a test should be an event. "I am not handing out your final. I am releasing your final, the way Pink Floyd released *The Dark Side of the Moon*. The way Spielberg released *Jurassic Park*." I have made such boasts to my students, and I have tried to back them up. Too often, teachers think of tests purely in terms of student accountability, as though tests were the primary tools available with which to keep students honest. No wonder so many students hate school. Most tests are simply IRS audits of the mind. Accountability may be necessary, but it does not contribute much to love. But what if the right test could make the world seem like a place rife with possibility, a place charged with theological energy? What if taking a test produced the kind of thrill which shot down your spine at the end of *The Matrix*? What if the teacher made it a goal to write a test which his students would remember until the day they died? What would become of the teacher who sat down to write a test while bristling with sheer Caesarean ambition?

Before I go on, allow me to ask: What kind of teacher did you want in high school? What kind of teacher might have set you on a path to higher, grander, intellectual things at the earliest possible age? What kind of teacher during freshman year might have convinced you to abandon the banalities of popular culture for purely pretentious reasons? If you could, as an adult, design the perfect teacher for your high school self, how would that teacher behave?

When I was in high school, I always wanted a teacher who was a bit like Robert Graves, some weirdo crypto-pagan whose affiliation with Christianity seemed so perilously unlike anyone else I knew, it was hard to credit his salvation. He might doubt my salvation, too, for that matter. I did. I wanted a wild teacher, a teacher in a rumpled linen suit who was hard to impress, never gave As, and who could quote from the book of Enoch. Someone with white hair who smelled like vetiver and cigarettes and exotic spices from the imported food he cooked in his cluttered apartment. I wanted a teacher who knew all the names of the archangels by heart, but had seen all the Jean-Luc Godard movies, too. I wanted someone who spoke frankly, but appreciatively, of women. A crooked poster of Arnold Böcklin's *Isle of the Dead* might hang on the wall of his office, and he would speak about Friedrich Nietzsche, Carl Jung, and Sigmund Freud as though they were all good fellows, very bright, but wrong about nearly everything. He would listen to Haydn, Rachmaninov, Debussy, drive an old boxy Volvo, mutter incoherently, laugh at all the wrong things, and sometimes fall to hysterics while listening to discussions of contemporary politics. An Easter and Christmas Christian who just happened to go to church every day of the year. I wanted a teacher who barely knew that he was teaching at all. I wanted someone who shouted, and was terrifying, but also harmless and friendly, because he feared God. Only I and one other student would like him, and rumors would swirl about him, and he would quit his job. In brief, I wanted a teacher with a batholithic personality, a personality so big I could unembarrassedly follow him. In the year 1997, when irony was pope and sarcasm emperor, I wanted someone to restore for me the awful and dread majesty of civilization.

I was scarcely into my third week teaching at a classical school when I realized that precious little was keeping me from becoming the teacher I had always wanted back in high school.

Here is the final assessment for my Medieval Humanities exam:

Step 1. One week prior to the final exam, inform students the final exam will be profoundly difficult and very long.

Step 2. Five days prior to the exam, purchase fifteen pounds of flour, a jar of yeast, and sea salt. Add water. Mix together. Let bread dough sit in fridge three days.

Step 3. Remind students again of how difficult the final exam will be. "You may bring all the books you read this year, though you will not know until the day of the test which of the books will be useful to you."

Step 4. Write a massive, unfinishable test. Here is the text of the Medieval Humanities exam which I handed out when students arrived for the exam:

> 1. *(20-line answer) Remembering is not easy. Remembering is difficult. Remembering takes work. Remembering the names of acquaintances, remembering anniversaries and birthdays, remembering passwords and codes . . . such remembering takes diligence. In prior years, upon arriving at the final exam of the year, I have asked students, "What will*

you remember from this class in five years?" Such a question assumes too much. Instead, this year, I would like you to reflect on the five things you learned this year that you would like to remember in the future.

Make a list of five items. Explain each item. Explain the importance of the thing, and how you want that thing you to change you.

What five things? Principles from books we studied. Chapters from books we studied. Lectures you have heard. Discussions we have had in class.

2. *(25-line answer) A good portion of this class has been devoted to the Last Judgement. The matter of the Last Judgement has been up for debate while reading the* Comedy, *but also in the final books of Augustine's* City of God. *There is some sense in which the school year is like life itself. At the end of the school year, you are judged. The summer is like the life to come. If you have worked diligently, the life to come will be pleasant. If you have not worked diligently, the Judgement will be a terror and the summer might see you performing additional work to atone for your failings during the school year.*

As such, what kind of final exam is appropriate to this class? What kind of final exam fairly judges the student? Describe a fitting, appropriate final exam for this class.

3. *(20-line answer) Governing yourself is hard. At fifteen or sixteen, you are already on your way to establishing certain vices as habits. You have some appreciation for how difficult it is to root out habitual vice. We often recognize too late what we should have been doing, or not doing, all along.*

However, in recognizing how hard it is to pursue virtue,

perhaps you have also had the thought that someday you will have children of your own, and you can set their lives up however you choose. It is hard to train a grown lion, but easy to train a little cub. Show me how much you have learned about self-government by describing particular habits you would like to inculcate in your own children.

Describe five habits or rituals you plan on instituting in the lives of your children which will help make them less susceptible to vice.

4. *(25-line answer) In Dante's vision of Hell, why are some sins punished more severely than others? Aren't all sins equal in God's eyes?*

5. *(25-line answer) Suppose for a moment that you are speaking with a student from this school who will be studying the* Comedy *next year. This student says, "I am not much interested in reading the* Purgatorio. *That's a book for Catholics. There is nothing about Purgatory in the Bible." What would you reply?*

6. *(25-line answer) Let us return to conversations we had much earlier this year about the Divine Nature. Christian metaphysics upholds the idea that God is omnipresent, omniscient, omnibenevolent, and omnipotent. Explain the relationship between God's omnibenevolence and His omnipotence. In what way is God's power intimately connected with God's goodness?*

7a. *Below you will find a series of claims which I would like you to mark True or False.*

a. _____*Only Christians can be good people.*

b. _____*The printing press, and the widespread distribution of cheap Bibles, has had absolutely no negative effects on modern American society whatsoever.*

c. _____*Faith is a virtue. A man is saved by faith, thus a man is saved by having virtue.*

d. _____*Most of what I believe about God has been gained not through conversations with friends, not through participation in church services, not through paying attention to sermons; rather, most of what I believe about God has arisen directly from personally reading the Bible.*

e. _____*God loves all men equally; the changeless nature of God means that He cannot love one man more than another.*

f. _____*I would like to be righteous.*

g. _____*I enjoy my life greatly primarily because I live when I do; the thought of living in the 1960s is somewhat horrifying to me.*

h. _____*In Hell, a man is punished for punishing himself.*

i. _____*Americans have crushed the problem of "works righteousness" with their profound devotion to entertainment, sports, and luxury; "works righteousness" may have been a problem in bygone eras, but we are flattering ourselves to pretend as though it is a real problem for us.*

7b. (25-line answer) *Choose one of the statements above and briefly explain your answer. Choose an item which is somewhat controversial. If you have marked an item True which most Christians would call False, explain why others are confused. If you have marked an item False which most Christians would call True, explain why others are confused.*

8. (20-line answer) *Let us say that five years from now, while*

attending college, you go on a first date to an art museum. While at the museum, you encounter Adriaen van de Velde's Annunciation. *As you have toured the museum, you and your date have made small talk about the paintings you see. Your date knows something about art and, not wanting to come off as uncultured, you want to say wise or learned things, as well. Record below five comments you might make about this painting which stand to impress your educated date.*

9. *(25-line answer) Ten years from now, you are married and have one little child. You work hard, do not make much money, and think fondly of your youth, when you had much time for leisure and study. Your average day involves nine hours of labor, though you are not yet in a career. You have a desk job, something just shy of what you studied in college, but if you are lucky, in two or three years the desk job will evolve into satisfying work. After nine hours of labor, you come home and cook dinner. You try to enjoy cooking dinner, but given how limited your paycheck is, you are not eating nearly so well as you ate in your parents' home. You are freshly amazed whenever you go to the grocery store at just how expensive food really is.*

Your parents still send you a nice check for your birthday (a hundred dollars), and with that money, you spend forty dollars on a babysitter, twenty dollars on two movie tickets, and twenty dollars on some coffee and dessert after the movie. The rest might go to a decent bottle of wine, or it might just go toward next week's food bill.

You have married someone you knew before you turned eighteen, just as your old literature teacher Mr. Gibbs suggested you would. Perhaps it is not someone from school, but a friend from outside school whom you didn't really know that well until after you graduated.

You attend a church which really isn't to your liking, but God did not create the world to satisfy you. Rather, He created you to satisfy Himself, and you resist the temptation to leave your church merely because you do not like the hymns they sing.

You enjoy your life, really, though you could not imagine finding such a life satisfying were someone to have told you about it ten years back. You have begun becoming like your parents, and you like it. One person you knew in high school has since died (the funeral, an impromptu class reunion two years ago). One has gone to jail. Half a dozen people you know have brazenly renounced the faith, though you are surprised by only one of these. This is the season of life in which wedding invitations come once a month.

In the midst of such a life, an old friend from high school sends you an email with a link to an essay contest sponsored by Veritas Christian School, a prestigious institution which has done well for itself over the years. All alumni are invited to write a one-thousand-word essay describing what exactly their classical education has done for them since high school. Was it worth it? Has it really mattered to you? On Facebook, you notice a few old acquaintances from school share links to the essay contest and make sarcastic remarks, like, "Nope. Latin is still a dead language," or, "All my classical education taught me to do was to judge people," or, "The school is willing to pay graduates to write propaganda for itself. How novel!" This strikes you as unfair, but these same people complained about having to tuck their shirts in back in ninth grade, so you are not terribly surprised. At the same time, plenty of students who hated school back in *ninth grade have gone on to achieve success and happiness, and they have surprisingly fond things to say of Veritas now that they don't have to go any longer.*

You write an essay. You submit it. A prize is promised to the winner, but the prize is undeclared. Your essay is about enjoying a small, unambitious life. A quiet life. Your Veritas education gave you the power to broker a deal with life which you find satisfying. In your essay, you describe cooking dinner for your family with less than luxurious ingredients. You describe how good those meals taste. Your essay wins the contest.

The prize is . . . surprisingly grand. Unpredictably lavish. You have won a seventy-five-thousand-dollar grant to take a year off from work and do one of the following:

a. Memorize the book of Ecclesiastes

b. Read through the entire ninth through twelfth Humanities curriculum (around twenty-five books, let us say)

c. Spend a year enrolled at École Grégoire-Ferrandi, one of the most prestigious culinary schools in Paris

d. Train to run a marathon

You must declare your intention at the beginning of the year, and shame forbids you from not following through with your declaration.

Which of these would you choose? Explain your answer.

10. (25-line answer) You have just been bitten by a spider on the foot. There is a 50 percent chance the spider bite will do nothing to you but hurt for a while, but there is also a 50 percent chance the spider which bit you was a Brazilian Wandering spider, and you will die within twenty minutes. The nearest hospital is half an hour away. Your friend tells you, "If you cut off your foot within the next five minutes,

the poison will not spread and you will not die!" You reply,
"But what if it's nothing? It may be nothing!" Your friend has
a machete in hand and is willing to cut off your foot. What
would Boethius tell you to do?

Step 5. On the day before the exam, print the unfinishable tests.

Step 6. On the day before the exam, bake thirty-one loaves of bread (sixteen ounces each), one loaf for each student.

Step 7. On the day of the tests, write the following message on the board: *Whatsoever a man sows, that shall he reap. Welcome to the Last Judgement.*

Step 8. Distribute tests. Tell students, "I want to read over the entire exam with you before you begin. It will be helpful for you to have the whole exam in your head. Part of your brain can be working on later problems while you are writing your answer to earlier questions."

Step 9. Read through entire exam (fifteen minutes just to read through exam).

Step 10. Tell students, "Do the first page first. After you do the first page, you may skip around. You have a little less than two hours to finish this. Good luck."

Step 11. Allow students twenty minutes to work.

Step 12. Once all students have finished the first page, the teacher exits room.

Step 13. While in a nearby room, the teacher dons black academic robes and a bishop's mitre and stole.

Step 14. From the next room, the bishop-teacher remotely begins blaring Ennio Morricone's "On Earth as It Is in Heaven" from massive hidden speaker inside the room where the students are taking the unfinishable test.

Step 15. Students look at one another confusedly.

Step 16. The bishop-teacher enters room.

Step 17. The bishop-teacher approaches a student in the front row, takes the unfinishable exam from him. The bishop-teacher detaches the first page of the test, hands back the first page only to the student. This page includes only the student's reflections on the five most important things he has learned over the year.

Step 18. The bishop-teacher says to class, "Do you want to take this exam?"

Step 19. The class loudly responds, "No."

Step 20. The bishop-teacher says, "Please remove the first page of the exam and fold it into thirds."

Step 21. The class removes the first page of exam and folds it into thirds.

Step 22. The bishop-teacher says, "Put this in your pocket. This is what you actually learned. My judgements of what you learned are ultimately meaningless."

Step 23. The bishop-teacher says, "Now bring me the rest of your massive unfinishable exams."

Step 24. One by one, the class approaches the bishop-teacher, and each student hands over their massive unfinishable exams.

Step 25. The bishop-teacher says, "Now everyone follow me!"

Step 26. The class processes to the school dumpster. The bishop-teacher says, "What do you believe?"

Step 27. The class recites the Nicene Creed while the bishop-teacher ceremonially throws massive unfinishable exams into dumpster, one by one.

Step 28. The class cheers when the last exam has been thrown away.

Step 29. The bishop-teacher says, "Now follow me."

Step 30. The class follows the bishop-teacher on foot to the bishop-teacher's home, which is on the campus of the school.

Step 31. The bishop-teacher momentarily enters his home while the class waits outside, then the bishop-teacher exits his home with thirty-one loaves of bread which are ceremoniously distributed to the thirty-one students.

Step 32. The class processes back to classroom.

Step 33. The class and bishop-teacher eat bread and butter and watch the classic French children's film *The Red Balloon* (1956). *Finis*

§

It might be argued that this assessment was not rigorous, and I would begrudgingly agree, but if we are interested in the test as a living and dynamic learning experience, we must ask: Would writing essays for two hours likely prove a greater spiritual help to these students over the long haul of their lives? What kind of learning metamorphoses the student? The patient and tedious work of, say, synthesizing Augustine's view of hell with Dante's view of hell, or in slowly unpacking Anselm's ontological argument until it makes sense—such work is part of this metamorphosis, but not the whole thing. A great many of the watershed moments of a human life are simply yielded to, submitted to, experienced in silence with delight. When I lead my sophomores on their spring trip to New York City to see the Metropolitan and the Cloisters, hear music performed at Carnegie Hall, and eat fine food, I say to them, "Soak it up. Don't try to say anything interesting about what you see, what you hear, what you taste. When we get back to the hotel at the end of the night, you can go to bed. There won't be a debriefing session where you have to pretend you understood it all. Just be grateful for it. Take in these good things, let your soul expand a little." Anyone who believes a trip to the Met would be more valuable if it were followed by a twenty-question quiz on the Robert Lehman Collection is mad.

Final assessment on Mary Shelley's Frankenstein

By the age of fifteen or sixteen, many teenagers have begun developing the ability to objectively criticize the way they are being raised (or the way they were raised as little children). I recall coming home from school when I was ten, watching cartoons all afternoon on television, and thinking, "This is very bad for me. When I have kids, I will not let them do this." The ability to criticize your own parents emerges from the need to criticize the parents of your peers. Every sophomore has a certain friend who isn't allowed to do anything, and every sophomore has a certain friend who is allowed to do everything. While a boy might express longing for libertine parents, he is also quietly disturbed by the fact that some parents don't really parent much. At sixteen, a boy is increasingly aware that the kind of people who beat their wives and go to jail come from somewhere, and that somewhere is more likely the home of recklessly permissive parents than moderate parents. Despite their curious conviction that most adults are good people, teenagers also spend enough time in the homes of their friends to know that some adults are complete idiots. Sixteen is not too young for a boy to begin considering how he will raise his own children and govern his own house. In fact, effective self-government depends on an ability to observe effective coercive government from without.

In my latter years as a teacher, I have become increasingly comfortable speaking of bad parenting from behind the lectern. Obviously, I don't name names, but my students are regularly amazed to hear the bizarre, outlandish defenses of bad behavior which I have collected in parent-teacher conferences over the years, not to mention the comments sections of articles I publish online. My approach to parent-teacher conferences has changed over the last decade, and I have become ever more incredulous of the slick, non-committal, overly diplomatic language which parent-teacher conferences sometimes seem to demand. "Problems" have largely become "struggles," "sins" have become "challenges," and every conversation must conclude with a generic hope or vaguely outlined confidence the year will turn out well.

In the first several years I taught, I was complicit in many such conversations with parents simply because they were far easier than speaking uncomfortable truths. Instead, I flattered, encouraged, and praised too much.

Once, while taking my sick daughter to a pediatrician, I realized the doctor was soft-peddling her health ("She'll be fine. Just a little . . .") to me the same way I soft-peddled the wit and wisdom of students to their parents. I had also lately read *The Death of Ivan Ilyich*, wherein Tolstoy lambasts professionals who employ greasy speech and an easy-going demeanor to slip past difficult human interactions. Around this same time, I began speaking with my priest about the sin of flattery, and he told me that some Church Fathers believed flatterers would be held accountable for the sins of those they flattered—if one man erected a false image of another man, he would be held responsible for the confusion and destruction caused by that false image.

Of course, flattering parents at conferences is profoundly dangerous to students. A child shirks responsibility, develops a reputation as a bully, always has an excuse, and yet mother and father come home from a meeting with the teacher to report, "He said you have some struggles, but who doesn't? Your teachers think it will be a great year." The bully has every right to be confused and horrified at this news. No one is going to stop him, and no one is even willing to try.

Sometimes a test is just as much for parents as it is for students:

By the latter half of Frankenstein, *Victor Frankenstein's behavior has been erratic for some time. His father Alphonse has noticed this but done little about it. Alphonse does not respond to Victor's bizarre mannerisms, his sudden trembling and shaking, but seems content to block out anything which does not comport with the* idea that the Frankenstein family is good, and that his children are well-adjusted. Alphonse has not been a tyrannical father, though he often sequesters himself off from the world, and he has sheltered his wife as though she were an "exotic flower" which cannot be troubled or inconvenienced by anything. The Frankenstein family is possessed of a number of irregularities (foremost, perhaps, the twenty-five-year age difference between Alphonse and his wife) and Alphonse does not want to hear the criticisms and questions of others, so he conducts his business in Geneva, yet he and his family live in relative isolation ten miles away. The Frankenstein family is so disinclined to honesty and transparency, Alphonse chooses a wife for his son when his son is just five years old and raises her as Victor's sister. Clearly, the Frankensteins want other people to stay out of their business. They are not open to criticism, rebuke, or advice. Alphonse and his wife are convinced they have done a fine job raising their children, and that is that.

And yet, shortly before Victor is to leave for England, Alphonse takes Victor's one friend aside and says, essentially, "My son should not be alone right now. His behavior is strange. Will you accompany him to England and keep an eye on him? I don't want to alarm Victor by making him feel as though he is being watched, but I fear Victor may become a danger to himself. Go with him, Henry. Act as his older brother. Shepherd him. Cheer him up. He is to marry in a year, and I want him in a good frame of mind when he takes his vows." Henry, of course, agrees. Given that Victor has secret business in England, having Henry as company throws a wrench in his plans. After they have travelled for some time, Victor begins acting moody once more and tells Henry that he needs a little time to himself. While Henry knows Victor is not well and has been charged to keep an eye on him, Henry is simply too much of a coward to tell Victor, "No. We must stay together. You are not well."

All throughout Frankenstein, *the characters are loath to ask one another difficult questions. Alphonse wants the lives of his family to pass easily, merrily, and difficult questions stand in the way of such ease. Rather, everyone is content to let others live however they like, keep as many secrets as they choose, not pry, not question, and not rebuke. The only character in the book who makes regular pleas for justice, fidelity, and integrity is deemed "a monster" and "a daemon." When Victor tells Henry he wants to go off on his own for a month or two, Henry does not ask Victor what he is going to do. This is the nature of their relationship. They allow one another to get away with everything, for this is easier than confrontation. Victor went to school in Geneva as a child, though, and one really must wonder what his teachers told his father. Unhappy, miserable, vicious, selfish adults like Victor Frankenstein do not suddenly come from nowhere. Such unhappiness and selfishness are years in the making. Of course, given Alphonse's insular approach to the world, we can imagine how he would respond to any criticism levelled against Victor by his teachers.*

Your task, then, is an unusual one. Imagine yourself as Victor's ninth-grade literature teacher. In ninth grade, Victor has already begun to show the signs and seeds of what he will become as an adult. You are an experienced teacher, though, and you have seen unhappy, miserable ninth graders become unhappy, miserable adults. You know that most parents do not like to hear bad news about their children, though it is sometimes necessary to give them such news. You also know there is an overly diplomatic language teachers are tempted to use, wherein they sheepishly try to inform parents of problems without hurting any feelings. Serious problems are couched in overly generic and innocuous terms, and every bit of bad news is balanced against two double helpings of good news, such that the bad news is easy to forget, or seems merely par for the course. On the other hand, you have also seen miserable ninth graders accept difficult news from teachers and parents, respond with humility, and alter their trajectory toward misery.

You must give Alphonse some troubling news about his son. Your task is to craft seven statements which address Victor's problems. Keep in mind that some of Victor's problems are his own, and some are borrowed from his parents. Often enough, criticizing Victor will mean criticizing Alphonse, as well. You are also going to speculate on ways Alphonse will try to deflect these criticisms, brushing them off as the ephemera of adolescence and no real concern. You must provide both the honest criticism and the deflecting response.

I will do the first one for you.

> *A. You say, "Victor does not willingly receive criticism on his work or his behavior. When he is rude to one of his fellow students and I correct him, telling him to be kind, he is stony, silent, and displeased. He does not readily agree that he ought to be kind. He receives correction as though it were a personal attack."*

> *B. Alphonse responds, "Victor has a very independent spirit. He needs to be given much room. He wants to take care of himself. When people criticize him, he feels as though he is being treated like a child."*

As for the erudition and quality of the work which I received in response to this assignment, I will say that my students had, for years, obviously been paying far closer attention to their parents and their friends' parents than anyone could have imagined.

CHAPTER SIX

A Coda: Math and Science,
Meet History and Literature

One of the most tantalizing possibilities of a daily catechism is the greater unity which might be shared between hard sciences and humane letters in classical schools. As it currently stands, old books play a dominant role in English, history, philosophy, Latin, Greek, and theology classes, but old books have little to do with math and science instruction. The power of philosophy is that it does not change, and the power of science is that it does, and so we should not be ignorant as to why Plato matters more to a modern ethics class than Heraclitus matters for a modern biology class.

Nonetheless, the science and math classes I took while attending a classical Christian school were densely packed with definitions and theories, but basically bereft of heroes. Many years after graduating high school, I read Thomas Kuhn's *The Structure of Scientific Revolutions* and found that science was far more of an art than I had ever imagined, and that scientific progress was no less dominated by desire, money, power, and creativity than were politics, religion, war, or epic poetry. Kuhn's account of science as a bloody, biased, relentlessly fallible human enterprise was a revelation to me and seemed nearly incompatible with science as I knew it. As I knew it, science was clean, neoclassically bright, never arbitrary, a Babel of facts ascending heavenward wherein each generation simply added a few more bricks to the top and could see just a touch further than their fathers. For Kuhn, science was high drama, replete with heroes and villains, and shortly after I finished his book, I read Peter Leithart's *Solomon among the Postmoderns*, which put theological and philosophical finishes on Kuhn's work.

A daily catechism has just as much to offer science and math teachers in the way of crowd control as it does history and literature teachers; however, a daily catechism could also go a long way in humanizing science for students. Students at classical schools understand the difference between hard and soft sciences, and they perceive the radical difference in the way both are assessed. A sophomore's second-period teacher insists on the superiority of old books, and yet his third-period teacher uses none. If science and math teachers have always wanted to include primary texts in their curriculums, and yet felt hamstrung by time or funds, a daily curriculum could incorporate lengthy quotes from Euclid, Pythagoras, Ptolemy, Kepler, Newton, Linnaeus, and Maxwell. There is currently a great need in classical math and science classrooms to bring in classical texts, and daily recitations from great mathematicians and scientists is the first step in normalizing what is old to disciplines which are centered on the new.

The school which began all classes—math, science, history, music, art, Latin, theology, and so forth—with catechesis would present a profoundly unified picture of learning and submission to students. Math would not be one kind of learning, and history another. Rather, students would receive daily confirmation that all subjects are human traditions, human endeavors, subject to human passions, and capable of divinity—as is appropriate to the work of God's image. Chemistry class might confirm literature class, and literature class confirm chemistry, if both began in humble submission to the masters. Open and direct reference to virtue, as well as vocal reverence for the canon, tradition, and Scripture are necessary on a daily basis in *all classes*.

For a moment, imagine the classical school where all classes began with a catechism. Consider the staggering volume of the canon which might be memorized before graduation. Imagine commencement ceremonies where the graduates could recite great literature and Scripture for an hour before receiving their diplomas. Imagine the weight of all that glory.

ABOUT THE PUBLISHER

The CiRCE Institute is a non-profit 501(c)3 organization that exists to promote and support classical education in the school and in the home. We seek to identify the ancient principles of learning, to communicate them enthusiastically, and to apply them vigorously in today's educational settings through curricula development, teacher and parent training, events, multimedia resources, and book publishing.

Learn more at www.circeinstitute.com or on Facebook or Instagram @circeinstitute.

ALSO AVAILABLE FROM CIRCE

How to Be Unlucky: Reflections on the Pursuit of Virtue by Joshua Gibbs

Tales of Wonder, Volume I

Tales of Wonder, Volume II

Mere Motherhood: Morning Times, Nursery Rhymes, and My Journey toward Sanctification by Cindy Rollins

A Handbook to Morning Time by Cindy Rollins

Hallelujah: A Journey through Advent with Handel's Messiah, by Cindy Rollins

The Lost Tools of Writing, Levels I, II, and III

The Journey Home: A Guide to Homer's Odyssey

The Space Between: A Guide to Homer's Iliad